AMERICAN SPUN

American Spun: 20 Classic Projects Exploring Homegrown Yarn
Copyright © One Peace Books, Inc.

ISBN 13: 978-1-935548-98-0

Author: Anna Sudo
Technical Editor: Chaitanya Muralidhara
Project Photography: Tsukuru Anderson
Modeling by: Greta Rose (pages: 11, 21, 25, 79, 83, 85, 101, 111, 117, 121, 131)
                 M'Lissa Hayes (pages: 17, 31, 41)
                 Norman Thomas (pages: 19, 47)
                 Hailey Inacio (pages: 55, 95)
                 Kristine Pool (pages: 14, 63)
                 Juniper Anderson (page: 35)

Photography by: Ami Volz (pages: title, 98, 99, 134)
                 Anita Fleming (pages: 6, 70, 71)
                 Soshi Sudo (page 7)
                 Jared Flood (pages: 8, 9)
                 Nicholas Colony (pages: 26, 27)
                 Manuosh, LLC (pages: 32, 33)
                 Cheyenne Grueb (pages: 38, 39)
                 Elsa Hallowell (pages: 44, 45)
                 Tamara White (pages: 53, 53)
                 Fancy Tiger Crafts (pages: 58, 59)
                 Debra Bohringer (pages: 64, 65)
                 Shannon Herrick (pages: 76, 77)
                 Spincylce Yarns, LLC (pages: 92, 93)
                 Krista McCurdy (pages: 108, 109)
                 Taylor Della Rocca (page: 118)
                 Jill Draper (page: 119)
                 Paula Farrar (pages: 128, 129)
                 Tsukuru Anderson (all other photography)

1234546789

One Peace Books
43-32 22nd Street #204 Long Island City, NY 11101 USA
http://www.onepeacebooks.com

Printed in the United States of America

AMERICAN SPUN

ANNA SUDO

ONE PEACE BOOKS

CONTENTS

Introduction   6

American Yarn Producer #01

BROOKLYN TWEED   8

Gannett   10
Monadnock   16
Colden   20

American Yarn Producer #02

HARRISVILLE DESIGNS   26

Moosilauke   28

American Yarn Producer #03

MANUOSH   32

Minnewaska   34

American Yarn Producer #04

MOUNTAIN MEADOW WOOL   38

Darton   40

American Yarn Producer #05

ELSAWOOL   44

Vallecito   46

American Yarn Producer #06

A WING & A PRAYER FARM   52

Harriman   54

American Yarn Producer #07

ELEMENTAL AFFECTS   58

Siyeh   60

American Yarn Producer #08

ROCK GARDEN ALPACA FARM   64

Chenago   66

American Yarn Producer #09

SHEEPS AND PEEPS FARM   70

Gauley   72

American Yarn Producer #10

FRABJOUS FIBERS   76

Groton   78
Winhall

American Yarn Producer #11

84

SPINCYCLE YARNS   92

Lummi   94

American Yarn Producer #12

LAKES YARN & FIBER   98

Coeur d'Alene   100

American Yarn Producer #13

PIGEON ROOF STUDIOS   108

Annadel   110
Umpqua   114

American Yarn Producer #14

JILL DRAPER MAKES STUFF   118

Rondout   120

American Yarn Producer #15

DONE ROVING YARNS   128

Sebago   130

Grafting   136
References & Resources   139

INTRODUCTION

My grandmother and I were skeptical. We were lost and the road was completely covered with water. The sudden rainstorm had flooded the little back roads with runoff from a nearby creek. I wasn't sure if my mother's little compact car would be able to make it through. There's a good reason people drive SUVs and pick-ups in the country. She decided to go for it and we slowly drove through the water. After a few tense moments, we made it through. Then, after a bit of bickering between my mother and her mother, we found our way home through the twisting roads of Southern Indiana. Washed out roads not withstanding, the day was clearing up nicely. We started with lunch at the Amish restaurant in Gosport and then perused the flea market next door. By chance on the way home we had spotted a sign for The Wee Sheep Farm yarn shop. Naturally, I had to check it out, and I was not disappointed. The store itself was stocked with both big-name yarns and an impressive selection of locally made yarns, and it was situated on a small farm with sheep, alpacas, and llamas. By the time we left, with a skein of shetland and a skein of alpaca in hand, the sun was finally shining. I felt that we'd stumbled upon a bit of heaven.

I've always considered knitting more of a journey than a destination. My reasoning is that it is often a significant investment of time, and there are many steps along the way before a project is finished. Step one—the discovery of a yarn. I can usually remember where all of my yarn came from. There is the sari silk yarn I bought at the weekend market in Bangkok, Thailand. There's the yarn I bought when I visited New York City to attend my friends' wedding. Then there are the four tiny skeins of silk that my husband and I hand-dyed using materials from the garden at Ock Pop Tok in Luang Prabang, and the local yarn I found in Georgetown, Colorado

(which we only discovered because I was carsick and when I opened the car door for a bit of fresh air there was The Quilted Purl).

The story behind finding the yarn gives the yarn a history —and the objects I make start with a history and meaning.

More and more, I find that the history of my yarn is important when I begin a new project. As all knitters know, it can take a significant amount of time to complete a project. Therefore I want the materials I use to have a history before they reach me, and on the other end of things, I want my finished piece to have a history after I have passed it along. All yarns have a history and a special path to the person who buys them. There is something intimate and satisfying about knowing a bit about who had a "hand" in making your yarn. When you knit with a yarn that is hand-dyed or hand-spun, you can see the hand of another maker in your work. I find it even more gratifying when I can find a yarn made by someone who knew the name of the animal that the fiber came from.

Why American yarns? The choice to feature American yarns is a function of two things—where I once was and where I am now. For the ten years previous to writing this book, I lived abroad. When I finally returned to the US in the spring, I returned with a desire to learn more about the huge fiber community here. To satisfy that desire, and to help my readers to the same, I wrote American Spun. I hope you enjoy the journey as much as I have.

Anna Sudo

American Yarn File #01

BROOKLYN TWEED

Portland, Oregon

Jared Flood

What led you to your current path?

Brooklyn Tweed began as a personal project; as my knitting skills developed, I began to understand what would be, for me, the perfect yarn, and I set out to make it. The uniqueness of our yarn comes partly from how it's spun; it is much lighter and airier than most yarns on the market, which is a combination of a woolen process (vs. a worsted spinning process), the amount of twist used in the yarn and the unique traits of the type of wool we use. Finding a sheep breed that would respond best to this technique took me to Wyoming, where I discovered the perfect balance between Columbia and Targhee sheep's wool that was springy and soft.

The other defining quality of our yarn is the color palette. Being a fleece-dyed yarn (wool is dyed prior to spinning then blended—like mixing paint) allows for a unique tweediness that accommodates the flecks of color that inflect the base tone. I have a background in oil painting, so this was especially exciting for me as it allows for the same kind of melding and mixing of complimentary and contrasting tones to create the perfect hue that resounds with richness and depth. When it is knitted, this tonality resonates across the garment, while maintaining a sophisticated subtlety.

What keeps you on this path?

The reception of our yarn, not only for its aesthetic qualities, but also its ethical background, keeps us motivated to face the challenge of producing American-made, sustainable yarn. When we started, the infrastructure for this kind of production seemed virtually nonexistent, as so much manufacturing has been outsourced overseas. It seems that people are beginning to pay attention to where their products—and within the knitting industry, their yarn—is coming from. This increasing focus on American made, breed-specific wool, as well as the distinctive properties of different kinds of yarn, motivates our persistent development and inspires us to continue doing what we do and developing new yarns that support more textile manufacturers in this country.

Project #01

GANNETT

Fingerless mittens

DETAILS

YARN

Brooklyn Tweed Loft (100% American wool, 275 yds / 251 m per 50g)
Color Fauna, 1 skein

FINISHED MEASUREMENTS

S (M, L)
Hand circumference: 6.5 (7.5, 8.5) inches
Cuff to fingers: 6.5 (6.5, 7.5) inches
Sample shown in M

RECOMMENDED NEEDLES

US size 4 (3.5 mm) needles, DPNs or long circular needles for magic loop

NOTIONS

Stitch holder, tapestry needle, stitch marker

GAUGE

24 stitches and 35 rounds = 4 inches x 4 inches in cable pattern

INTRODUCTION

Cables really stand out in this yarn, so I chose to use this simple stitch pattern to accent these mitts. The warm colors remind me of autumn and kicking through piles of dried leaves.

PATTERN

Both mitts are worked identically.

Cast on 40 (44, 52) sts, pm, and join in the round.

Setup Round: (k1, p1) around.
Repeat previous round 4 more times.

Work Rounds 1-12 of the Cable Pattern once.

Thumb Gusset

On the following rounds, you will increase sts for the Thumb Gusset at the beginning of the round. Continue to work the appropriate round of the Cable Pattern over the remaining sts as indicated.

Round 1: M1, pm, work Cable Pattern to end. 1 st increased

Round 2: k1fb, sm, work Cable Pattern to end. 1 st increased

Round 3: k1, p1, sm, work Cable Pattern to end.

Round 4: M1p, k1, p1, M1, sm work Cable Pattern to end. 2 sts increased

Rounds 5-6: (p1, k1) to marker, sm work Cable Pattern to end.

Round 7: M1, (p1, k1) to marker, M1p, sm, work Cable Pattern to end. 2 sts increased

Round 8-9: (k1, p1) to marker, sm, work Cable Pattern to end.

Round 10: M1p, (k1, p1) to marker, M1, sm, Cable Pattern to end. 2 sts increased

Rounds 11-12: (p1, k1) to marker, sm work Cable Pattern to end.

Size S only

Work rounds 7-12 once more.
Then work rounds 7-9 one last time. 54 sts

Size M only

Work rounds 7-12 two more times. 60 sts

Size L only

Work rounds 7-12 two more times.
Then work rounds 7-9 one last time. 70 sts

Thumb separation (all sizes)

Round 1: Place the 14 (16, 18) thumb sts onto a stitch holder, rm, cast on 2 sts, continue working in Cable Pattern to end.

42 (46, 54) sts

Slip the first cast on stitch so that it becomes the last stitch of the round.

Sizes S (M,-) only

Round 2: k2tog, (p2, k2) to last 4 sts, p2, ssk. 40 (44,-) sts

Size L only

Round 2: p2tog, (k2, p2) to last 4 sts, k2, ssp. 52 sts

Hand (all sizes)

Continue working in Cable Pattern as follows:

Size S only

Work Round 11-12 of Cable Pattern, then work Rounds 1-10 one final time.

Size M only

Work Rounds 3-10 of Cable Pattern.

Size L only

Work Rounds 5-12 of Cable Pattern, then work Rounds 1-10 one final time

All sizes

Next Round: (k1, p1) around.

Repeat previous round 4 more times.

Bind off all sts in pattern.

Thumb

Return the 14 (16, 18) thumb sts to the needles. With RS facing, rejoin yarn and pick up and knit 2 sts in the crook of the thumb, over the cast on stitches. Arrange the two picked up sts so that the first picked up st becomes the last st of the round and the second picked up st becomes to first st of the round. 16 (18, 20) sts.

Sizes S (-,L) only

Round 1: Sl1 (the cast on st), k1, *p1, k1, repeat from * to last 2 sts, ssp. 15 (-, 19) sts
Round 2: k2tog, p1, (k1, p1) to end. 14 (-, 18) sts

Next Round: (k1, p1) around.

Repeat previous round 9 (-, 11) more times.

Size M only

Round 1: Sl1 (the cast on st), p1, *k1, p1, repeat from * to last 2 sts, ssk. 17 sts
Round 2: p2tog, k1, *p1, k1, repeat from * to end. 16 sts

Next Round: (p1, k1) around.

Repeat previous round 10 more times.

All Sizes

Bind off all sts in pattern. Weave in all ends and block.

Cable Pattern

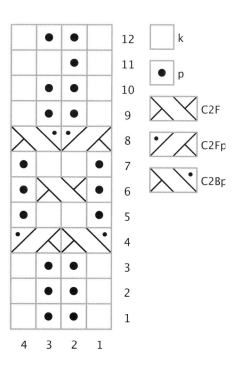

(worked in the round over a multiple of 4 sts)

Round 1: k1, (p2, k2) to last 3 sts, p2, k1

Rounds 2-3: Same as Round 1

Round 4: *C2Fp, C2Bp, repeat from * to end

Round 5: p1, (k2, p2) to last 3 sts, k2, p1

Round 6: p1, *C2F, p2, repeat from * to last 3 sts, C2F, p1

Round 7: Same as Round 5

Round 8: *C2Bp, C2Fp, repeat from * to end

Rounds 9-12: Same as Round 1

Project #02

MONADNOCK

Chevron Rib Hat

DETAILS

YARN

Brooklyn Tweed Loft (100% American wool, 275 yds/251 m per 50g)
Color Tent, 1 skein

FINISHED MEASUREMENTS

S (M, L)
Circumference: 16 (18, 20) inches at brim, unstretched
While choosing a size, keep in mind that brim will stretch 1-2"
Sample shown in M

RECOMMENDED NEEDLES

US size 4 (3.5 mm) needles, 16-inch circular and DPNs, or long circular
needles for magic loop

NOTIONS

Tapestry needle, stitch markers

GAUGE

22 stitches and 38 rounds = 4 inches x 4 inches in (k1, p1) ribbing

INTRODUCTION

This woolen-spun yarn is light and warm. The tweed highlights suggest a grassy field flecked with deep oranges and reds—an element I wanted to accentuate with the design, that resembles rolling foothills to my eye.

PATTERN

Cast on 80 (96, 112) sts, place marker, and join in the round.

Setup round: (k1, p1) around.
Repeat previous round eight more times.

Next round: *(k1, p1) 8 times, pm, repeat from * around.

Work rounds 1-17 of Chevron Ribbing pattern four times total. On Round 17 of the final repeat, remove markers as you come to them.

Crown decreases

Remove marker and slip the first st of the round to the right hand needle so that it becomes the last st of the round just knit, pm for new beginning of round.

Round 1: *(p1, k1) 3 times, k2tog, repeat from * around. 70 (84, 98) sts

Round 2: *(p1, k1) 3 times, k1, repeat from * around.

Round 3: *(p1, k1) twice, p1, k2tog, repeat from * around. 60 (72, 84) sts

Round 4: (p1, k1) around.

Round 5: *(p1, k1) twice, k2tog, repeat from * around. 50 (60, 70) sts

Round 6: *(p1, k1) twice, k1, repeat from * around.

Round 7: *p1, k1, p1, k2tog, repeat from * around. 40 (48, 56) sts

Round 8: Same as round 4.

Round 9: *p1, k1, k2tog, repeat from * around. 30 (36, 42) sts

Round 10: *p1, k2, repeat from * around.

Round 11: *p1, k2tog, repeat from * around. 20 (24, 28) sts

Round 12: Same as round 4.

Round 13: k2tog around. 10 (12, 14) sts

Round 14: k all sts around.

Round 15: k2tog around. 5 (6, 7) sts

Finishing

Break yarn and pull through the remaining sts and secure. Weave in all ends and block.

Chevron ribbing

(worked in the round over a multiple of 16 sts)

Round 1: *(k1, p1) 3 times, k3, (p1, k1) 3 times, p1, sm, repeat from * around.

Round 2: *(k1, p1) twice, k1, (k1, p1) twice, k2, (p1, k1) twice, p1, sm, repeat from * around.

Round 3: *k1, p1, k2, (p1, k1) 4 times, k1, p1, k1, p1, sm, repeat from * around.

Round 4: *k2, (p1, k1) 6 times, k1, p1, sm, repeat from * around.

Rounds 5-9: (p1, k1) around.

Round 10: (p1, k1) twice, (p1, k2) twice, (p1, k1) 3 times, sm, repeat from * around.

Round 11: *(p1, k1) twice, k1, (p1, k1) 3 times, k1, (p1, k1) twice, sm, repeat from * around.

Round 12: *p1, k2, (p1, k1) 5 times, k1, p1, k1, sm, repeat from * around.

Round 13: *(k1, p1) 7 times, k2, sm, repeat from * around.

Rounds 14-17: (k1, p1) around.

Project #03

COLDEN

Headscarf

DETAILS

YARN

Brooklyn Tweed Loft (100% american wool, 275 yds / 251 m per 50g)
Color Wool Socks, 1 skein

FINISHED MEASUREMENTS

M (L)
5.75 inches x 28 (30.5) inches
To fit head circumference 18 (20.5) inches
Sample shown in M

RECOMMENDED NEEDLES

US size 4 (3.5 mm) needles

NOTIONS

Tapestry needle, stitch marker

GAUGE

22 stitches and 38 rows = 4 inches x 4 inches in (k1, p1) ribbing
24 stitches and 35 rows = 4 inches x 4 inches in Chart A

INTRODUCTION

This pattern is a bit of retro fun—as sweet as the strawberry motif running its length. The tweedy yarn and ruddy color give it a heirloom feel. Perfect for a spring day at the market.

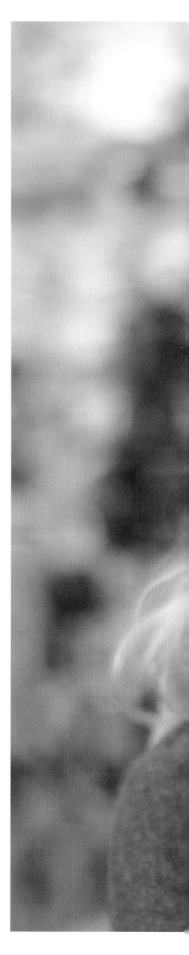

PATTERN

First Tie

Cast on 5 sts.

Row 1 (RS): (k1, p1) twice, k1.

Row 2 (WS): (p1, k1) twice, p1.

Row 3: k1, p1, M1, k1, M1, p1, k1. 7 sts

Row 4: k1, p1, k3, p1, k1.

Row 5: k1, p1, k1, M1p, k1, M1p, p1, k1. 9 sts

Row 6: (p1, k1) 4 times, p1.

Row 7: (k1, p1) twice, M1, k1, M1, (k1, p1) twice. 11 sts

Row 8: (p1, k1) twice, p3, (p1, k1) twice.

Row 9: (k1, p1) twice, k1, M1p, k1, M1p, k1, (k1, p1) twice. 13 sts

Row 10: (p1, k1) 6 times, p1.

Row 11: (k1, p1) 6 times, k1.

Repeat rows 10-11 sixteen more times, then work row 10 one final time. Piece should measure 5 inches from cast on.

Work rows 1-18 of Chart A once. 37 sts

Work rows 1-8 of Chart B once.

Work rows 1-24 of Chart C three (four) times. On each row, the stitches outlined in red will be repeated 4 times.

Work rows 1-36 of Chart D once. 29 sts

Work rows 1-12 of Chart E once. 13 sts

Second Tie

Row 1: (k1, p1) 6 times, k1.

Row 2: (p1, k1) 6 times, p1.

Repeat rows 1-2 seventeen more times.

Row 3: (k1, p1) twice, k1, CDD, k1, (p1, k1) twice. 11 sts

Row 4: (p1, k1) twice, p3, (k1, p1) twice.

Row 5: (k1, p1) twice, CDD, (p1, k1) twice. 9 sts

Row 6: (p1, k1) 4 times, p1.

Row 7: k1, p1, k1, CDD, k1, p1, k1. 7 sts

Row 8: p1, k1, p3, k1, p1.

Row 9: k1, p1, CDD, p1, k1. 5 sts

Row 10: (p1, k1) twice, p1.

Finishing

Bind off all sts in pattern.

Weave in all ends and block.

☐	k on RS p on WS	╱	k2tog
●	p on RS k on WS	╲	ssk
Ⴑ	k1tbl on RS p1tbl on WS	⋀	CDD
◯	yo	☐	pattern repeat
ⅴ5	1into5	▧	no stitch

Chart A

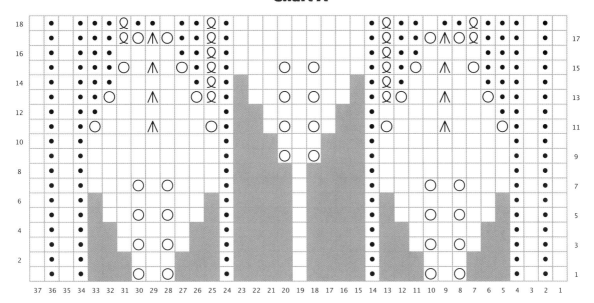

Chart B

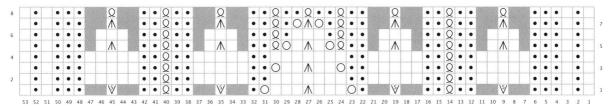

Chart C

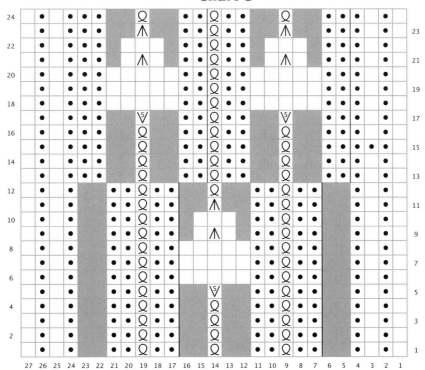

23

Chart D

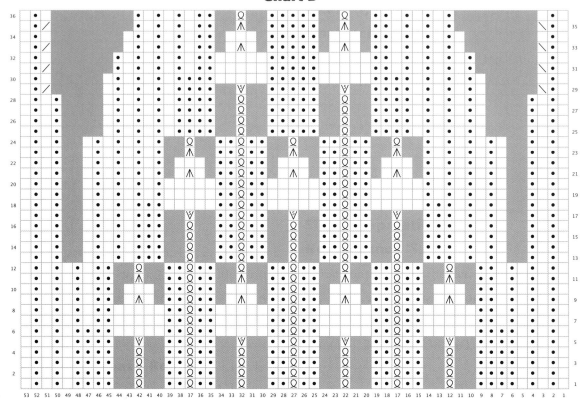

Chart E

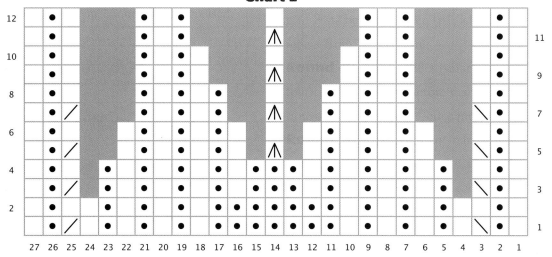

	k on RS p on WS		/	k2tog
•	p on RS k on WS		\	ssk
Ω	k1tbl on RS p1tbl on WS		Λ	CDD
O	yo			pattern repeat
V5	1into5			no stitch

American Yarn File #02

HARRISVILLE DESIGNS

Harrisville, New Hampshire

Nicholas Colony

What led you to your current path?

We started Harrisville Designs in the spring of 1971 after the 120 year old woolen mill in our small town closed in October, 1970. The 20th century had skipped over Harrisville as the village was so self-contained and off any beaten path. In 1970 it was in a remarkable state of preservation and was considered the only early textile village that had survived in its original form. Textiles seemed to be over, not just in Harrisville, but in most of New England as well. Harrisville Designs was established with the single goal of sustaining textile production in a village where it had thrived since the 1790's. In 1977, the entire village was designated a National Historic Landmark.

Any interesting anecdotes?

While we pride ourselves in offering consistent and dependable yarns of a high quality, it is also fun to spin special yarns for particular projects. We have spun yarns in the past that have ended up in a cape that was featured in the movie *Back to the Future Part 2*, in blankets in the movie *Amistad* and in the officers' uniforms in the movie *Master and Commander*. In each case the task was to reproduce a yarn from a sample that was over a hundred years old.

What keeps you on this path?

Harrisville Designs plays a critical role in the preservation of the village and the fact that yarns are still spun here helps tell the story of the early nineteenth century when industrial production was in its infancy. As long as the business can stand on its own financial legs, we are happy that it can contribute to the future of the village and to the understanding of its past.

What would you like people to know about your process?

We take great care in being small enough to be flexible and large enough to spin yarn on an economical basis. We spin yarns for our open lines that are sold to knitters and weavers around the world and we also do custom yarns for special projects. We are known for our heathered lines that are achieved by blending Dyed in the Wool colors carefully and consistently.

Project #04

MOOSILAUKE

Scarf

DETAILS

YARN

Harrisville Designs WATERshed
(100% wool, 110 yds/100 m per 50 g)
MC: 945 Farwell, 3 skeins
CC: 965 Driftwood, 2 skeins

FINISHED MEASUREMENTS

11 inches width x 50 inches length

RECOMMENDED NEEDLES

US size 9 (5.5 mm) needles, 40-inch circular, for main body
Two US size 7 (4.5 mm) needles, 40-inch circular, for ribbing

NOTIONS

Tapestry needle, stitch markers

GAUGE

18 stitches and 28 rows = 4 inches x 4 inches in slipped stitch X pattern
with larger needles
16.5 stitches and 27 rounds = 4 inches x 4 inches in (k1, p1) ribbing
with smaller needles

Introduction

This yarn is substantial, cushy, and warm—all of which are things I look for in the perfect chunky winter scarf. The dynamic, graphic pattern is fun to knit and wear. Bury your face in this to stave off the winter chill.

PATTERN

Note: This pattern requires the use of a steek technique. See Resources section (page 139) for recommended resources on making a steek.

With larger needles and CC yarn, cast on 215 sts, place marker, and join in the round. From this point, CC and MC will be alternated on each round. Odd-numbered rounds are worked in CC, and even-numbered rounds are worked in MC.

Round 1 (CC): p1, k around.
Round 2 (MC): p1, k2, pm, k to last 2 sts, pm, k2.

Slip-Stitch Chart

You will now begin working from the Slip-Stitch Chart in between markers. On each round, the sts outlined in red will be repeated 17 times.

Round 3: p1, k2, sm, work Round 1 of Slip-Stitch Chart, sm, k2.
Rounds 4-22: Continuing as above, work through Rows 2-20 of Slip-Stitch Chart.
Rounds 23-50: Continuing as above, repeat rounds of Slip-Stitch Chart 7-20 two more times.
Rounds 51-55: Continuing as above, work through Rows 21-25 of Slip-Stich Chart.
Round 56: p1, k2, remove marker, k to next marker, remove marker, k2.
Round 57: p1, k around.

Bind off all stitches.

Steek

Using your preferred steeking method, create steek next to the purl stitch column at the beginning of the round. Cut through the purl column.

Ribbed Stitch Border

With smaller needles and MC yarn, start at either the cast on or bind off edge and *working along the length of the scarf, pick up and knit 192 sts. To evenly distribute sts across the edge, pick up 9 sts for every 10 sts until you have a total of 192 sts. Pm and turn work, pick up and knit 34 sts along one steeked edge and pm. To evenly distribute sts across the edge, pick up 3 sts over 5 rows as follows, pick up one st per row for 2 rows, skip one row, pick up one st for one row, skip one row. Pm, turn work and repeat from * once more. Join to work in the round. 452 sts

Round 1: *k1, yo, p1, (k1, p1) to marker, yo, sm, repeat from * three more times. 8 sts increased (1 yo on either side of the corner sts)
Round 2: *k1, k1tbl, p1, (k1, p1) to 1 st before marker, k1tbl, sm, repeat from * three more times.
Round 3: *k1, yo, (k1, p1) to 1 st before marker, k1, yo, sm, repeat from * three more times. 8 sts increased
Round 4: *k1, p1tbl, (k1, p1) to 2 sts before marker, k1, p1tbl, sm, repeat from * three more times.

Rounds 5-8: Work Rounds 1-4 once more. 16 sts increased.

Bind off all sts in pattern.

Finishing

Weave in all ends and block to measurements.

MC

CC

k on RS
p on WS

sl1

RSST

LSST

SSRC

pattern repeat

row repeat

Slip-Stitch Chart

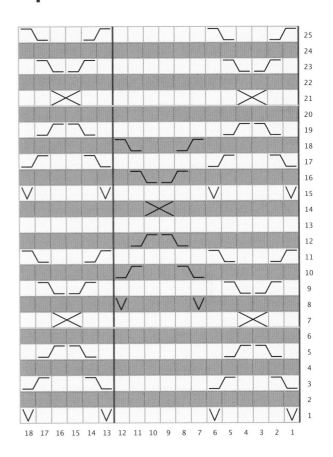

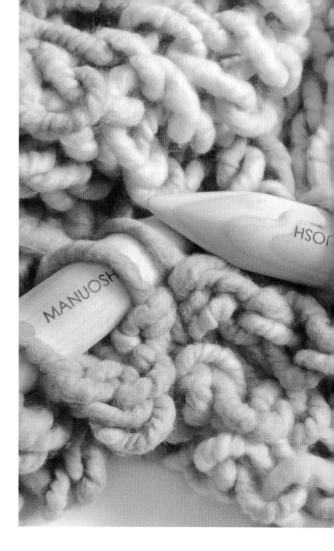

American Yarn File #03

MANUOSH

Manhattan, New York

What led you to your current path?

Manuosh is a brand based upon community and sustainability, while still maintaining timeless aesthetics. From day one, we wanted to create fun, chic, and glamorous knit products for the modern day knitter made in an eco-friendly manner In the USA. This ideal flows through our "Hand made with love" philosophy, from our mega yarn in a rainbow of color-ways, Glam knitting needles filled with glitter, to our playful knitwear and knit patterns—all items are handcrafted from start to finish, with love. Our products reflect our curious and optimistic approach to the world, and we like to think of ourselves as the "Willy Wonka" of yarn, little surprises at every stitch.

Knitting has been a part of way of life for centuries. Its about going back to the basics—using natural & renewable products, ones hands, and creating timeless, beautiful pieces that are made with love. Knitting is a souvenir of craftsmanship, a record of time and creativity.

What would you like people to know about your process?

Manuosh yarns have been handcrafted from start to finish and are utterly unique. We love natural fibers and primarily use merino wool in our yarns. Our wool fibers are from the Hudson Valley and the American South, where we choose the best quality available. All wool used by Manuosh is ethically, and cruelty-free produced & sourced. Our fibers are hand-dyed in small batches using natural dye—and our dye lots are small and unique. The beauty of the colors we achieve is directly related to the small size of the lots we dye. Once fibers have been dyed they are then spun into yarn–which is enormously time intensive. To spin one skein of our yarn, it takes in excess of an hour. Even though the raw materials are the same, no two skeins are completely alike because of their handmade nature. Each skein is truly individual and one-of-a-kind.

Project #05

MINNEWASKA

Pudgy Blanket

DETAILS

YARN

Manuosh Pudgy (100% merino wool) This yarn is sold in 200 yard skeins or 30 yard skeins
C1: Spice, 1 skein (200 yds)
C2: Brown Sugar, 2 skeins (60 yds)
C3: Chili, 1 skein (30 yds)

FINISHED MEASUREMENTS

42 inches square

RECOMMENDED NEEDLES

US size 50 (25 mm) needles

NOTIONS

2 stitch markers, felting needle (optional)

GAUGE

3 stitches and 6 rows = 4 inches x 4 inches in stockinette stitch
(Gauge is not critical for this project but will affect yardage)

Introduction

This Manuosh yarn is like knitting with marshmallow. The fabric is dense, yet soft and squishy, making the perfect blanket for curling up on the couch when weather turns wet. The super bulky yarn leads to a sensation of instant gratification—and luxury.

PATTERN

With C1, using the crochet cast on method, cast on 55 sts.

Row 1: sl1 knitwise, k to end.
Rows 2-4: Repeat row 1

Break yarn and switch to C2.
Row 5 (RS): k25, pm, k1, CDD, k to end. 53 sts
Row 6 (WS): sl1, k2, p to last 3 sts, k3.
Row 7: sl1, k to 1 st before marker, pm, CDD (remove previous stitch marker), k to end. 2 sts decreased.
Row 8: Same as row 6.
Rows 9-10: Repeat rows 7-8. 49 sts

Break yarn and switch to C1.

Row 11: k to 1 st before marker, pm, CDD (remove previous stitch marker), k to end 47 sts
Row 12: sl1, k2, p to last 3 sts, k3
Rows 13-14: Repeat rows 7-8. 45 sts

Break yarn and switch to C3.

Rows 15-16: Repeat rows 11-12. 43 sts

Break yarn and switch to C1.

Rows 17-18: Repeat rows 11-12. 41 sts

Rows 19-48: Repeat rows 7-8 fifteen more times. 11 sts

Row 49: sl1, k3, CDD, k to end, removing markers. 9 sts
Row 50: sl1, k2, p3, k3.
Row 51: sl1, k2, CDD, k to end. 7 sts
Row 52: sl1, k2, p1, k3.
Row 53: sl1, k1, CDD, k2. 5 sts
Row 54: sl1, k1, p1, k2.
Row 55: sl1, CDD, k1. 3 sts
Row 56: sl1, k2.
Row 57: CDD.

Break yarn and pull through remaining st.

Finishing

Since this is super bulky yarn, instead of weaving in ends, I chose to knot the ends. Then I used a felting needle to slightly felt the knots so that they would not come undone. You may choose to weave in ends or knot them as I did.

Block to finished measurements.

American Yarn File #04

MOUNTAIN MEADOW WOOL

Buffalo, Wyoming

What led you to your current path?

Mountain Meadow Wool Mill was opened in 2007. Karen Hostetler and Valerie Spanos opened the mill with the purpose of sustaining the beautiful sheep ranches of the American West. Many of the sheep ranches were started 100 years ago by Basque immigrants who came here from Spain and France to be shepherds. Some of this heritage remains but much is disappearing. The wool from this area is fine and soft and comes mostly from Rambouillet, Merino, Targhee and Columbia sheep. Our intent was to create a "brand identity" for this beautiful Wyoming wool by processing the wool near the farms. We were the first US mill to provide consumers with traceability of the yarn back to the ranch.

What do you want people to know about you?

The love of the wonderful fiber and yarn and the impact the mill is beginning to make on the family ranches in the state. We want people to be able to connect with these wonderful sheep ranchers and the lifestyle that still exists out on the plains and mountains of Wyoming.
Valerie and I have many stories along the path of creating this mill.

Any fun anecdotes?

When we first started spinning yarn we had so much trouble—it felt like we were up to our knees in fiber wrecks from the spinner! We put in a 911 call to our wool processing expert and he was soon on his way to assist us. The first thing he said was the wool was too short in staple length but we just looked at him and said "we have 20,000 lbs of that exact wool so we HAVE to make it work!" So many hours later and many experiments later we finally found a solution for OUR wool. Yeah! We still keep some skeins of the first wool we successfully spun.

—Karen Hostetler

Project #06

DARTON

Triangle Shawl

DETALS

YARN

Mountain Meadow Wool Cody
(100% wool, 200 yds/ 183 m per 50 g),
Color Dark Grey, 2 skeins

FINISHED MEASUREMENTS

39 inch wingspan x 20.5 inches from center neck to point

RECOMMENDED NEEDLES

US size 6 (4 mm) needles

NOTIONS

Crochet hook, waste yarn, tapestry needle, stitch marker

GAUGE

18.5 stitches and 34 rows = 4 inches x 4 inches Right chart pattern
(Gauge is not critical for this project but will affect yardage)

Introduction

Simple and not too fussy, this is a great shawl to wear whenever the occasion calls for an extra bit of warmth. Nubbly and soft, this yarn has an impressive bounce, and is a dream against the skin.

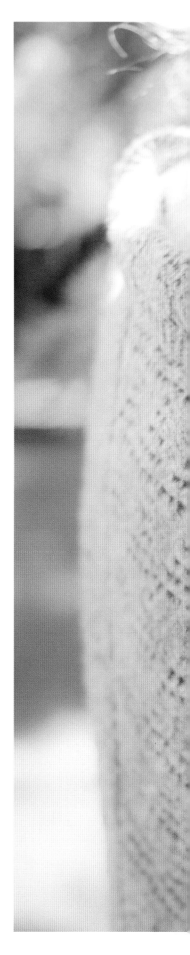

PATTERN

Cast on

With the waste yarn and crochet hook, chain 3 sts. Using working needles and main yarn, pick up and knit 1 st each in the 3 bumps on the crochet chain. Work 7 rows in garter stitch pattern (knit each row).

Setup Row (RS): k3, turn work 90 degrees, pick up and knit 3 sts along the side of the piece (one in each garter ridge), turn work 90 degrees, unravel the crochet provisional cast on and place the 3 sts on the needle, k3. 9 sts

Next Row: k3, pm, p1, pm, p1, pm, p1, pm, k3.

Body

Row 1 (RS): k3, sm, yo, k to marker, yo, sm, k1, sm, yo, k to marker, yo, sm, k3. 4 sts increased

Row 2 (and all WS rows until Row 10): k3, sm, p to last marker, sm, k3.

Rows 3-10: Repeat Rows 1-2 four more times. 29 sts

Begin working Logwood pattern, following the charts:

Row 11 (RS): k3, sm, work Row 1 of Right Chart, sm, k1, sm, work Row 1 of Left Chart, sm, k3.

Row 12 (WS): k3, sm, work Row 2 of Left Chart, sm, p1, sm, work Row 2 of Right Chart, sm, k3.

Rows 13-20: Continuing as above, work through Rows 3-10 of Right Chart and Left Chart. 49 sts

Rows 21-80: Work Rows 11-20 six more times. 169 sts

Garter Border

Row 1: k3, sm, yo, k to marker, yo, sm, k1, sm, yo, k to marker, yo, sm, k3. 173 sts

Row 2: k3, sm, k to next marker, sm, k1, sm, k to next marker, sm, k3.

Rows 3-16: Repeat Rows 1-2 seven more times. 201 sts

Finishing

Bind off all sts loosely, using a larger needle if necessary. Weave in ends and block.

☐	k on RS / p on WS
◯	yo
╱	k2tog
╲	ssk
☐	repeat
▨	no stitch

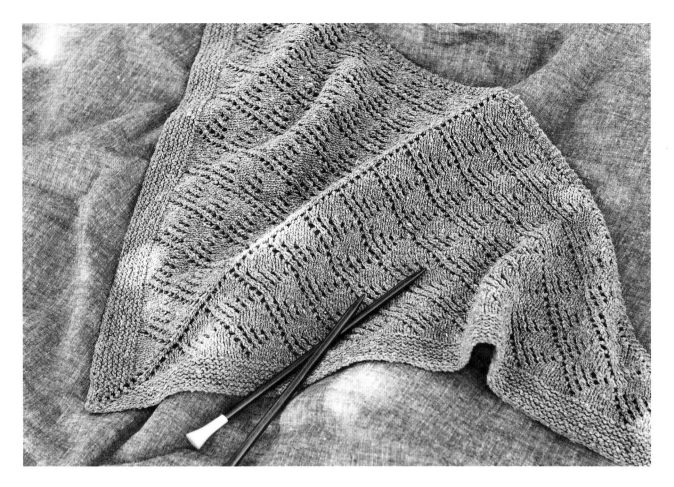

Right chart

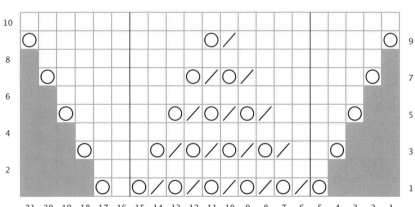

Left chart

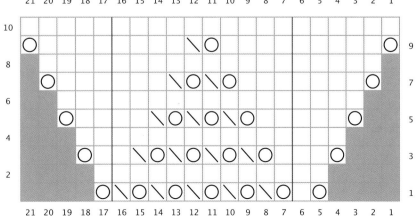

American Yarn File #05

ELSAWOOL

Bayfield, Colorado

Elsa Hallowell

What led you to your current path?

Animals always have been a big part of my life. I was raised on a farm and spent many happy hours with sheep, goats, horses, dogs, cats, and other creatures. Later, I managed a pet farm and worked as a veterinary nurse. Arts and crafts have also played had a prominent role in my life—it was in the 70's that I became particularly interested in fiber crafts. Eventually these two lifelong interests converged into a career of raising fiber animals and designing and selling animal fiber products.

In 1983 I bought some Angora goats and some sheep, and soon had 200 - 300 fiber animals on my ranch. In 1986 I met a flock of Cormo sheep and fell in love with this magnificent breed. By the early 90's my entire flock consisted of purebred Cormo sheep. After a few years, one of my white ewes gave birth to a black ram, who later was bred to a large number of my ewes. Within a few years, black sheep comprised a third of my flock. By this time I was having my wool made into yarns and finished goods, and Green Canyon Ranch was on its way to becoming Elsawool.

Almost 30 years later I lost my flock to OPP. I miss my beautiful Cormos, but I'm thankful that I'm able to buy excellent quality Cormo wool. Every spring, after the family who own the sheep harvest and bag the wool, I buy the wool, ship it to Texas to be washed, ship the washed wool to woolen and worsted spinning mills to be spun into different kinds of yarns, and have some of the yarns knitted into clothing.

What would you like people to know about your process?

I want people to know that I care. I'm serious about the quality of the products and service offered by Elsawool. I also want people to know that I value everyone who's a part of Elsawool—each member of the family who cares for the sheep and harvests the wool, each person who helps to wash the wool, each person who helps to spin the wool, each knitter, each person who helps to prepare the yarn and finished goods for sale, each person who helps to sell the products, each customer, and many others. All of us together keep the cycle alive and thriving.

I am very thankful for everyone who's a part of this circle called Elsawool.

Project #07

VALLECITO

Mens Sweater

DETAILS

YARN

ElsaWool Company Woolen Spun Worsted Weight
(100% cormo wool, 113 g, 237 yds /216 m)
Color white/dark brown marled
4 (5, 5, 6, 6, 7, 7, 8) skeins

FINISHED MEASUREMENTS

S (M, L, XL, 2X, 3X, 4X, 5X)
Finished chest: 37 (41, 45, 49, 53, 57, 61, 65)
To fit chest: 34 (38, 42, 46, 50, 54, 58, 61) inches
Sample shown in S

RECOMMENDED NEEDLES

US size 8 (5 mm) needles, 32-inch circular, and DPNs or long circular
needles for magic loop

NOTIONS

Tapestry needle, stitch markers, 2 stitch holders or waste yarn

GAUGE

18 stitches and 25 rounds = 4 inches x 4 inches in stockinette stitch

Introduction

*This sweater is designed in a relaxed-fit style for kicking back on
the porch on cool Saturday mornings, a mug of coffee in hand and a
crossword awaiting your attention. Elsa's wool is durable, strong—
and incredibly soft.*

PATTERN

Neck

Cast on 84 (86, 88, 90, 92, 94, 96, 98) sts, pm, and join in the round.

Round 1: k all sts.
Round 2: p all sts.
Repeat rounds 1-2 three more times.

Setup round: *k10 (8, 8, 6, 4, 2, 2, 0), pm, (k1, p1) four times, k16 (19, 20, 23, 26, 29, 30, 33), (p1, k1) four times, pm, repeat from * once more.

Yoke

Round 1 (Increase Round): *LLI, k to marker, RLI, sm, (k1, p1) four times, k1, LLI, k to 9 sts before marker, RLI, k1, (p1, k1) four times, sm, repeat from * once more. 8 sts increased.

Round 2: Work all sts in pattern (knit the knit sts, purl the purl sts as they appear).

Repeat the last two rounds 16 (18, 22, 24, 27, 30, 32, 34) more times.
220 (238, 272, 290, 316, 342, 360, 378) sts

Sizes S (M, -, -, -, 3X, 4X, 5X) only
Final Increase Round: *k to marker, sm, (k1, p1) four times, k1, LLI, k24 (27, -, -, -, 43, 47, 52), M1, k to 9 sts before marker, RLI, k1, (p1, k1) four times, sm, repeat from * once more. 6 sts increased
226 (244, -, -, -, 348, 366, 384) sts

Sizes - (-, L, XL, 2X, -, -, -) only
Final Increase Round: *k to marker, sm, (k1, p1) four times, k1, LLI, k to 9 sts before marker, k1, (p1, k1) four times, sm, repeat from * once more. 2 sts increased
(-, 274, 292, 318, -, -, -) sts

Work 20 (19, 15, 12, 10, 5, 7, 5) rounds in pattern.

Sleeve Separation Round

Next Round: *Slip 44 (46, 54, 56, 60, 64, 68, 70) sts onto a stitch holder, cast on 14 (16, 18, 20, 20, 20, 22, 24) sts, sm, work in pattern to next marker, sm, repeat from * once more.
166 (184, 202, 220, 238, 260, 274, 292) sts

Body

Round 1: *p to marker, sm, (k1, p1) four times, k to 8 sts before marker, (p1, k1) four times, sm, repeat from * once more.
Round 2: *(p1B, p1) to marker, sm, (k1, p1) four times, k to 8 sts before marker, (p1, k1) four times, sm, repeat from * once more.
Round 3: *(p1, p1B) to marker, sm, (k1, p1) four times, k to 8 sts before marker, (p1, k1) four times, sm, repeat from * once more.

Repeat rounds 2-3, 42 (44, 47, 48, 50, 51, 53, 54) more times.

Split hem

Setup: Remove beginning of the round marker, (p1B, p1) 3 (4, 4, 5, 5, 5, 5, 6) times, p1B 1 (0, 1, 0, 0, 0, 1, 0) time, pm to mark the new beginning of the round.

On the next round, remove all markers except for the beginning of the round marker.

Round 1: k all sts.
Round 2: p all sts.
Repeat rounds 1-2 three more times.

From this point the sweater will be worked flat.

Front Split Hem

Setup Row: k 83 (92, 101, 110, 119, 130, 137, 146) sts, place the remaining sts onto waste yarn or stitch holder.

Work in garter stitch (knit each row) for 11 more rows.
Bind off all sts.

Back Split Hem

Place 83 (92, 101, 110, 119, 130, 137, 146) sts from waste yarn or stitch holder onto a needle.
Work in garter stitch (knit each row) for 11 more rows.
Bind off all sts.

Sleeves

Left sleeve

Pick up and knit 14 (16, 18, 20, 20, 20, 22, 24) sts from the underarm cast on edge, place the 44 (46, 54, 56, 60, 64, 68, 70) sts from the stitch holder on to a needle and knit all sts from the needle, pm, and join in the round.
58 (62, 72, 76, 80, 84, 90, 94) sts

Work 42 (33, 21, 46, 54, 44, 44, 38) rounds in stockinette stitch (knit each round).

Sleeve decreases

Decrease Round: k2tog, k to last 2 sts, ssk. 2 sts decreased

Continuing in stockinette stitch, repeat Decrease Round every 6 (6, 6, 4, 4, 4, 4, 4) rounds, 8 (10, 13, 15, 14, 16, 18, 20) more times.
40 (40, 44, 44, 50, 50, 52, 52) sts

Work 5 (5, 5, 3, 3, 3, 3, 3) rounds in stockinette stitch.

Cuff

Next round: (k1, p1) around.
Repeat previous round 17 more times.
Loosely bind off all sts in pattern.

Right Sleeve

Place the 44 (46, 54, 56, 60, 64, 68, 70) sts from the stitch holder on to a needle and knit all sts from the needle, pick up and knit 14 (16, 18, 20, 20, 20, 22, 24, 27) sts from the underarm cast on edge, pm and join in the round.
58 (62, 72, 76, 80, 84, 90, 94) sts

Work the remainder of the sleeve like same as left sleeve.

Finishing

Weave in all ends and block according to the schematic.

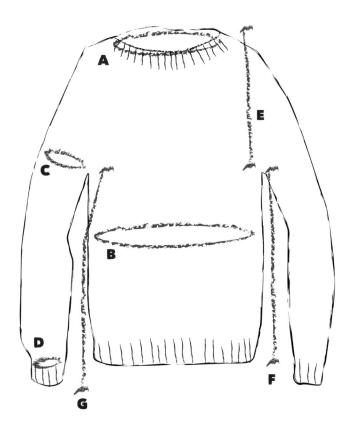

A: 18.5 (19, 19.5, 20, 20.5, 21, 21.5, 22) inches

B: 37 (41, 45, 49, 53, 57, 61, 65) inches

C: 13 (14, 16, 17, 18, 19, 20, 21) inches

D: 9 (9, 10, 10, 11, 11, 11.5, 11.5) inches

E: 10.25 (10.75, 11.25, 11.5, 12.25, 12.25, 13.25, 13.5) inches

F: 17 (17.5, 18.5, 19, 19.5, 20, 20.5, 21) inches

G: 19 (19.5, 20.5, 21, 21.5, 22, 22.5, 23) inches

American Yarn File #06

A WING AND A PRAYER FARM

Shaftsbury, Vermont

Tamara White

What led you to your current path?

Originally the farm began as a product of the family's child-led interests combined with home education and the best land stewardship of our property in Southern Vermont. However, as the fiber flock grew through the years and the family became more knowledgeable about raising grazing and browsing animals, more fences were built and a barn replaced the original 2-sided shed. The permanent structures made expanding the flocks and breeding easier to accommodate and thus supported growth.

The alpacas, Angora goats, and Cotswold, Cormo & Merino sheep, were added to the flocks through the years either by being placed on the farm for sanctuary or acquired to contribute to a fiber recipe for a variety of yarns. The Angora goats' locks are silky Mohair that blends beautifully with the Cormo and also Cotswold for a drapey, soft yarn. The Merino is colored, dark brown, and blends well with the black alpaca for a soft, strong yarn. The Cotswold fleeces are a handspinners' delight with long staple, stunning crimp, soft yarns.

All of our lambs and kid goats are born here on the farm and we have been able to be present for nearly all of the births. Every animal has a name, so every yarn has a name. For example, you can use yarn called "Milkweed, Lavender & Hester" for the combination of Milkweed, the Angora goat, and Lavender & Hester, the two Cotswold ewes. You might also spin from a roving combination of the Shetlands' Ruva & Rupert's wool plus alpacas' Indy & Hayden's fiber. You could knit with yarn from Shetlands' Nikki, Ninian & Nessa and make a lovely fawn-colored sweater. They are a family of like-fleeced Shetland sheep because they are mother and children.

There is little free time because of the number of livestock which require attention in some way or another. Seasonally, the jobs change and are easier in some ways, more difficult in others. There is no "quiet time" to speak of. Each day is full.

You can buy Wing and a Prayer yarn from Woolful.com or from the Wing & A Prayer Farm online mercantile at wingandaprayerfarm.com.

Project #08
HARRIMAN

Embroidered Brim Hat

DETAILS

YARN

MC: Woolful Mercantile Shetland-Mohair-Merino
(23% Shetland/27% Merino/50% Mohair, 120 yds / 110 m per 76 g)
Color Ash, 1 (2, 2) skein(s)

CC: Woolful Mercantile Shetland-Mohair
(47% Shetland/53% Mohair, 120 yds / 110 m per 76 g)
Color Oat, 1 skein (About 30-40 yds will be used for embroidery)

FINISHED MEASUREMENTS

S (M, L)
Circumference: 16 (18, 20) inches at brim, unstretched
While choosing a size, keep in mind that brim will stretch 1-2"
Sample shown in S

RECOMMENDED NEEDLES

US size 7 (4.5 mm) needles, 16-inch circular and DPNs, or long circular needles for magic loop

NOTIONS

Tapestry needle, stitch marker, stitch holder

GAUGE

18.5 stitches and 25 rounds = 4 inches x 4 inches in (k1, p1) ribbing

Introduction

What makes this yarn so luscious is the blend of shetland, mohair, and merino. The shetland and merino give it softness, while the mohair creates a halo—making this hat warm, cozy, and plush.

PATTERN

To make it easier to embroider the pattern onto the hat, the embroidery pattern set-up is knit into the fabric in the form of yarn-overs and purl bumps.

With MC, cast on 76 (84, 92) sts, place marker, and join in the round.

Rounds 1-8: (p1, k1) around.
Rounds 9-11: k all sts around.
Round 12: *k2tog, yo, repeat from * around.

Rounds 13-16: Repeat rounds 9-12.
Rounds 17-19: Knit all sts around.
Round 20: (p1, k1) around.

Continue working in (p1, k1) ribbing until the hat measures 8 inches from cast on.

Crown Decreases

Round 1: *p1, k1, k2tog, repeat from * around. 57 (63, 69) sts
Round 2: (p1, k2) around.
Round 3: (p1, k2tog) around. 38 (42, 46) sts
Round 4: (p1, k1) around.
Round 5: k2tog around. 19 (21, 23) sts
Round 6: k all sts around.
Round 7: k2tog to last st, k1. 10 (11, 12) sts

Break yarn, pull through remaining stitches and secure. Weave in all ends.

Brim Embroidery

Hold hat with the crown to your left. Cut a 72-inch length of CC yarn (join additional lengths of yarn as needed). Thread the yarn through the tapestry needle and pull it so that the ends of the yarn are even. You will be using two strands of yarn for each embroidery stitch.

Step 1: Starting from the inside of the hat, insert the tapestry needle into a yarn over (1a) located in the left column of yarn overs and pull the yarn most of the way through, leaving a small tail on the inside of the hat.

Next, count four rows above the yarn over and pick up both legs of the first purl stitch (1b) on the right side and pull yarn through. Return needle to the yarn over (1a) and pull through.

Make sure to keep the stitches loose so that they can stretch with the brim when the hat is worn.

Step 2: Insert the tapestry needle into the yarn over (2a) directly to the right of the one just worked and pull yarn through.

Next, count four rows above the yarn over and pick up both legs of the first purl stitch (2b) on the left side and pull yarn through. Return needle to the yarn over and pull through.

Continue working Steps 1 and 2 around the hat.

When pulling the tapestry needle through the yarn overs, make sure that the strands from the stitch previously worked are held above the yarn over. This ensures that the stitch currently being worked will over lap the stitch previously worked.

When working Step 2 for the final time, before picking up both legs of the purl stitch, slide the tapestry needle under the strands of the very first stitch. Pick up both lefts of the purl stitch and before returning the needle to the yarn over, slide the tapestry needle under the strands of the first stitch. Return needle to yarn over.

Finishing

Secure all embroidery ends and block.

Brim Embroidery Charts

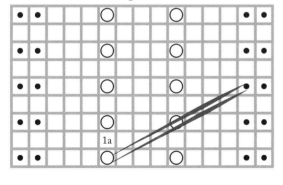

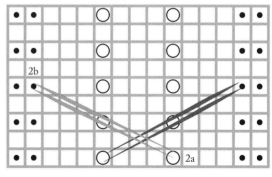

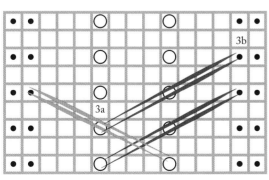

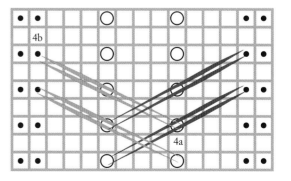

k   • p   ◯ yo

American Yarn File #07

ELEMENTAL AFFECTS

Desert Hot Springs, California

Jeane deCoster

What led you to your current path?

Years of other things. I pursued knitting, weaving and spinning as passionate hobbies for many years while following a semi-conventional professional path. I hopped about from Fashion Design to Garment/Textile Manufacturing to Information Technology for 20+ years.

Throughout my corporate professional life, I persisted in learning more about 'why and how' things worked together to become yarn. As things changed in both my career and my life, an opportunity to leap into the unknown arrived—a chance to follow my simmering desire to design yarn for a living. And I took it.

What would you like people to know about your process?

It takes a lot of work to create apparently simple, quality products for the general knitting market. It is a fine line to maintain quality that reflects the origins of the materials and the small batch nature of the product while still meeting the expectations of hand-knitters everywhere.

It is a specific goal of mine to source all of my breed-specific wool directly from the growers/breeders here in the U.S.—and use our rapidly diminishing manufacturing resources to make the yarn. I have learned a lot about blending the cycles of nature with the commercial demands of our on-shore manufacturing resources. It is an ongoing challenge that I enjoy every day.

What keeps you on this path?

Both the process and the raw materials fascinate me—it feels like creating something from almost nothing. Or better yet, the whole process from raw wool to dyed yarn is almost like alchemy to me. Once you add color—well, there's nothing like seeing the endless variety of beautiful things you can make from what, essentially, starts out as small bits of fluffy gray stuff.

I also love how working with these materials makes me feel, and how those feelings are reflected outward to others—hence the odd combination of words used for my company name: Elemental Affects.

Can you tell us about your Heirloom Romney Yarn?

Until recently, most hand knitters tended to expect very soft yarns when shopping at their local yarn stores. When I first developed the Romney yarn, we had very few yarn stores that understood the wide variety of what wool yarn could, and should, be.

Fancy Tiger Crafts in Denver, Colorado is a leader in how to successfully educate their customers about a variety of wool yarns and how yummy (and useful) they can be. We collaborated on the color range and they have taken over the work of branding, styling and telling the story of this wonderful yarn.

Project #09

SIYEH

Slipper Socks

DETAILS

YARN

Fancy Tiger Crafts Heirloom Romney
(100% Romney wool, 200 yds /182 m per 113 g)
Color Huckleberry, 2 skeins

FINISHED MEASUREMENTS

M (L)
Calf circumference: 14 (15.75) inches
Foot circumference: 8.5 (9.5) inches
Foot length: 10 (11) inches
Sample shown in M

RECOMMENDED NEEDLES

US size 7 (4.5 mm) needles, DPNs, or long circular needles for magic loop

NOTIONS

Fiber Trends Suede 2-piece slipper bottoms (1 pair) , cable needle, tapestry needle, stitch markers

GAUGE

17.5 stitches and 24 rounds = 4 inches x 4 inches in stockinette stitch

Introduction

This line of vibrantly colored yarns is so much fun that it can be hard to choose between them. I chose Romney Yarn for these slipper-socks as it creates a durable and beautiful garment—made even more long-lasting with leather patches on the pads of the feet.

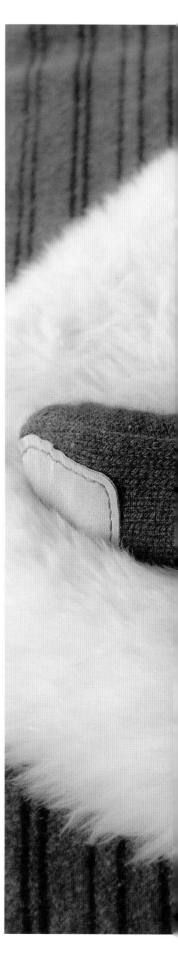

PATTERN

Both socks are worked identically.

Cuff

Cast on 64 (72) sts, pm, and join in the round.

Next Round: (k1, p1) around.

Repeat previous round 7 more times.

Round 1: k4, pm, p to last 4 sts, pm, k4.

Rounds 2-4: k4, sm, p to marker, sm, k4.

Round 5: C4F, sm, ssp, p to 2 sts before marker, p2tog, sm, C4B. 2 sts decreased

Rounds 6-7: k4, sm, p to marker, sm, k4.

Round 8: k4, sm, ssp, p to 2 sts before marker, p2tog, sm, k4. 2 sts decreased

Round 9-10: k4, sm, k4, sm, p to marker, sm, k4 .

Work rounds 5-10 five (six) more times. 40 (44) sts

Round 11: C4F, sm, ssp, p to 2 sts before marker, p2tog, sm, C4B. 38 (42) sts

Rounds 12-16: k4, sm, p to marker, sm, k4.

Round 17: C4F, sm, p to marker, sm, C4B.

Round 18: k4, rm, p to marker, rm, k4.

Round 19: k2, C3F, p28 (32), C3B, k2.

Round 20: k5, p28 (32), k5.

Round 21: k3, C3F, p26 (30), C3B, k3.

Round 22: k6, p26 (30), k6.

Round 23: k4, C3F, p24 (28), C3B, k4.

Round 24: k7, p24 (28), k7.

Round 25: k5, C3F, p22 (26), C3B, k5.

Round 26: k8, p22 (26), k8.

Round 27: k6, C3F, p20 (24), C3B, k6.

Round 28: k9, p20 (24), k9.

Round 29: k7, C3F, p20 (22), C3B, k7.

Round 28: k10, p 18 (22), k10.

Size M

Proceed to Short Row Heel.

Size L only

Round 29: k8, C3F, p- (20), C3B, k8.

Round 30: k11, p- (20), k11.

Proceed to Short Row Heel.

Short Row Heel

Setup Round: k10 (11) sts, p18 (20), pm to mark the new end of the round.

The sock will now be worked flat.

Row 1 (RS): k19 (21), W&T.

Row 2 (WS): p18 (20), W&T.

Row 3: k to 1 st before wrapped st, W&T.

Row 4: p to 1 st before wrapped st, W&T.

Repeat rows 3-4 five more times.

Row 5: k6 (8), lift the wrap off of the next st and place it on the needle, knit the next stitch and the wrap together, W&T (this is the second wrap on this st).

Row 6: p7 (9), lift the wrap off of the next st and place it on the needle, purl the next stitch and the wrap together, W&T (This is the second wrap on this st).

Row 7: k to the next wrapped st, lift both wraps onto the needle and knit them together with the next st, W&T.

Row 8: p to the next wrapped st, lift both wraps onto the needle and purl them together with the next st, W&T.

Repeat rows 7 and 8 four more times.

Row 9: k18 (20), lift the wrap off of the next st and place it on the needle, knit the next stitch and the wrap together, W&T (this is the first wrap on this st)

Row 10: p19 (21), lift the wrap off of the next st and place it on the needle, purl the next stitch and the wrap together, slip round marker, W&T (this is the first wrap on this st), replace round marker.

Foot

From here, the sock will be worked in the round.

Round 1: k20 (22), lift the wrap off of the next st and place it on the needle, purl the next stitch and the wrap together, p16 (18), lift the wrap off of the next st and place it on the needle, purl the next stitch and the wrap together.

Round 2: k20 (22), p18 (20).
Repeat round 2 until the foot measures 7.75 (8.75) inches from the back of the heel.

Rounds 3-4: Knit around.

Toe Decreases

Round 1: (k1, k2tog, k14 (16), ssk) twice. 34 (38) sts

Rounds 2 and all even rounds: k all sts around.

Round 3: (k1, k2tog, k12 (14), ssk) twice. 30 (34) sts

Round 5: (k1, k2tog, k10 (12), ssk) twice. 26 (30) sts

Round 7: (k1, k2tog, k8 (10), ssk) twice. 22 (26) sts

Round 9: (k1, k2tog, k6 (8), ssk) twice. 18 (22) sts

Round 11: (k1, k2tog, k4 (6), ssk) twice. 14 (18) sts

Finishing

Use the Kitchener stitch to graft the first 7 (9) sts to the last 7 (9) sts. Weave in all ends and block.

After blocking, pin slipper bottom pieces onto the bottom of the socks and sew on using your preferred method.

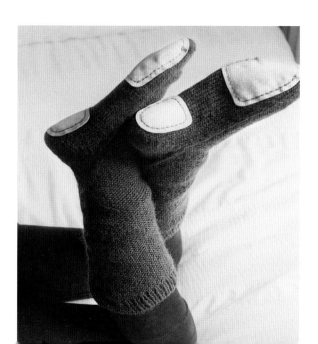

American Yarn File #08

ROCK GARDEN ALPACA FARM

Oxford, New York

Debra Bohringer

What led you to your current path?

My husband and I retired from our previous business and love the outdoors and nature so we decided we needed to fill our time with something that we could enjoy. Someone had told us about alpacas and it seemed to be a great option for us. I am now spending my time with my animals and exploring and learning all the things that can be done with their wonderfully soft fiber!

What keeps you on this path?

The alpacas! I absolutely love them and their fiber right from shearing to sorting to washing, picking and processing, whether it be done at a Mill that I send some of my sorted fiber to or processed by myself. I have acquired my own carding machine, wet felting machine, and e-spinner and am looking into spinning wheels. I dye fiber, nuno felt, needle felt, spin, and hope to be able to actually knit with some of my home spun in the future when I have time to learn. Right now I simply enjoy looking at the skeins hanging in my farm store. I wanted to be able to share my alpaca fiber with other fiber artists and that is why I opened my Rock Garden Alpacas Fiber Store.

More than anything else, I simply love creating things!

Project #10

CHENANGO

Rug

DETAILS

YARN

Rock Garden Alpacas Alpaca Bulky/Rug Yarn
(100% alpaca fiber spun around a cotton core, 52.5 oz., 125 yds)
Color medium rose gray, 1 skein

FINISHED MEASUREMENTS

40 inches height, 44 inches diameter

RECOMMENDED NEEDLES

US size 50 (25 mm) needles, 40-inch circular and DPNs

NOTIONS

Crochet hook, waste yarn, tapestry needle, 10 stitch markers

GAUGE

3 stitches and 3.5 rounds = 4 inches x 4 inches in stockinette stitch
3 stitches and 4 rounds = 4 inches x 4 inches in garter stitch
(Gauge is not critical for this project but will affect yardage)

Introduction

Delightfully fuzzy, soft, and rich, this yarn knits into a timeless accent for your home. Designed especially for curling up with a good book and a cup of tea by the fire, this rug makes any room feel like home.

PATTERN

Cast on

With the waste yarn and crochet hook, chain 3 sts. Using the working needle, leave a yarn tail of at least 8 inches, pick up and knit the 3 bumps on the crochet chain. Place marker, and join in the round. 3 sts

Round 1: (k1, yo) around. 6 sts
Round 2: (k1, k1tbl) around.
Round 3: Same as Round 1. 12 sts
Round 4: (k1, p1tbl) around.

Petal Chart

Work rounds 1-14 of Petal Chart. On each round, the chart sts will be repeated 6 times. 96 sts

Bind off all sts knitwise.

Finishing

Undo the crochet cast on and thread the yarn tail through the live stitches. Pull the yarn tight to close the hole. Weave in all ends and block.

Petal Chart

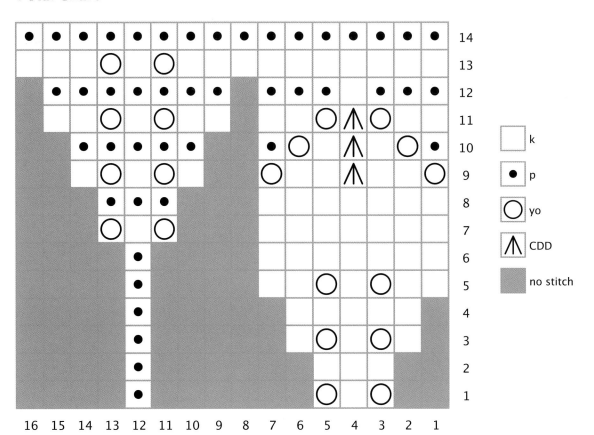

American Yarn File #09

SHEEPS AND PEEPS FARM

Aurora, West Virginia

Anita Fleming

What led you to your current path?

As we tend to our flock of longwool sheep on our fifth-generation family farm, we are driven by a love of our animals and a great sense of stewardship for the land that sustains them. The fact that we have the opportunity to produce our own yarn is an added bonus, as we love to knit!

What keeps you on this path?

Each season brings excitement and sense of rhythm to life. We love watching our sheep turn the pasture grass into soft, beautiful curly locks of wool.

What would you like people to know about your process?

We strive to work in a natural and sustainable manner following the rhythms of the seasons. 'From sheep to shawl', we love every step of the process that produces our wool and yarn.

Our favorite time of year is lambing in the spring. We love that moment when a newborn lamb hits the ground in a sloppy little heap. It lifts and shakes its little head, and then we hear the gasp of that first breath. Still after hundreds of times, we feel the thrill of having witnessed a miracle... Each and every time... A true miracle.

Project #11

GAULEY

Jelly Jar Cozies

DETAILS

YARN

Sheeps and Peeps Millspun Longwool
(100% farm grown wool, 4.24 oz/120 g, 250 yds/228m)
C1: Camo (gold), 1 skein
C2: Oh Ruby! (pink), 1 skein
Each cozy uses one of the yarns (C1 or C2) as the main color, and the
other as the contrast color, and vice versa

FINISHED MEASUREMENTS

12 oz. Jelly Jar (Pint Jar)
Circumference: 8.25 (10.25) inches
Height [lip of jar to base]: 5.75 (5.75) inches

RECOMMENDED NEEDLES

US size 6 (4 mm) needles, DPNs or long circular needles for magic loop

NOTIONS

Tapestry needle, stitch marker

GAUGE

20 stitches and 27 rounds = 4 inches x 4 inches in stockinette stitch

Introduction

*On a cool Autumn evening, there's nothing quite like filling these up
with some hot apple cider and a splash of cinnamon whiskey. I love
how lustrous this yarn is and it has tons of character.*

PATTERN

Note: To make it easier to work the herringbone embroidery stitch onto the covers, the embroidery pattern set-up is knit into the fabric in the form of purl bumps.

With main color, cast on 40 (50) sts, place marker, and join in the round.

Next round: (k1, p1) around.
Repeat previous round three more times.

Work 2 rounds in stockinette stitch (knit all sts).

Charts
Work rounds 1-12 of either Chart A or Chart B.

Work 12 rounds of stockinette stitch.

Decreases
Round 1: *k2tog, k2 (3), repeat from * to end. 30 (40) sts
Rounds 2, 4, 6: k all sts around.
Round 3: *k2tog, k1 (2), repeat from * to end. 20 (30) sts
Round 5: *k2tog, k0 (1), repeat from * to end. 10 (20) sts
Round 7: k2tog around. 5 (10) sts

Pint Jar Only
Round 8: k all sts around.
Round 9: k2tog around. 5 sts

Break yarn and pull through remaining sts. Weave in ends.

Embroidery
Chart A
Holding the jar cover so that the opening is at the top, begin work. Cut a long length of contrast color yarn (Join additional lengths of yarn as needed). Thread the yarn through the tapestry needle and pulling it so that the ends of the yarn are even. You will be using two strands of yarn for each embroidery stitch.

Step 1: Starting from the inside of the cover, insert the tapestry needle into the fabric on the left side of the purl stitch marked 1a and pull through. Leave a small tail on the inside of the cover. Insert the needle on the right side of the purl stitch marked 1b. The needle is now on the wrong side of the work.

Step 2: Insert the tapestry needle into the fabric on the left side of the purl stitch marked 1b and pull through. Insert the needle on the right side of the purl stitch marked 2a.

Continue working in the manner of Steps 1 and 2 around the cover.

Finishing
Weave in all ends and block.

Chart A Embroidery

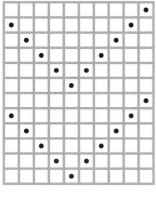
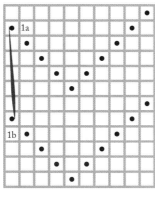
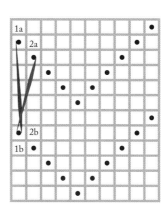

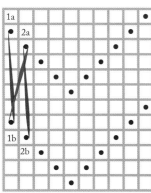
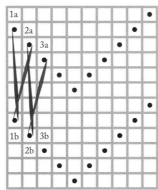

Legend:
- ☐ k
- ● p

Chart B Embroidery

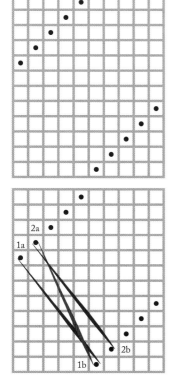
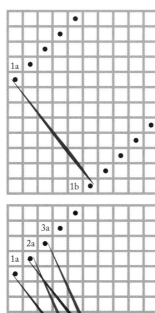
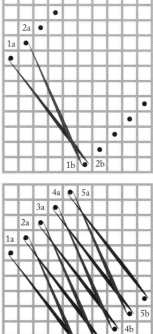

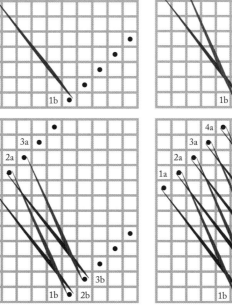

American Yarn File #10

FRABJOUS FIBERS

Brattleboro, Vermont

Frabjous Fibers is a business with humble beginnings, born from a love of textiles and fiber arts and built on a desire to create a healthy work/life balance steeped in color and texture. What started as a one-woman import business structured to support worker cooperatives in Nepal that made yarns from recycled sari silk has grown, over nearly a decade, into so much more. Working with beautiful yarns led to spinning, and spinning led to fiber dyeing, and fiber dyeing led to yarn dyeing, and now Frabjous Fibers and Wonderland Yarns creates hundreds of unique products in-house in southern VT, from hand dyed top for spinners, to luxurious, richly-hued hand dyed yarns in soft merino and lustrous silk.

What keeps you on this path?

We love what we do! Our work environment is fun, flexible, and likely the most colorful place in town. Our team is a family, and we support each other in the ongoing creative process. We are never short of ideas for new colors or products, so the path goes ever onward.

What would you like people to know about your process?

We dye our fibers and yarns in small batches with loving care and attention, using special techniques we've developed over years working with the best possible materials. We really went down the rabbit hole using Alice in Wonderland as inspiration for our yarn line, as there are always new colors and combinations in the works!

—Shannon Herrick

Project #12

GROTON

Fingerless Mittens

DETAILS

YARN

Wonderland Yarn Mad Hatter
(100% superwash merino wool, 113g, 344yds/314m)
Color 11 Looking Glass, 1 skein

FINISHED MEASUREMENTS

S (M, L)
Hand circumference: 6.5 (7.5, 8.5) inches
Cuff to fingers: 8.5 (9, 9.5) inches
Sample shown in M

RECOMMENDED NEEDLES

US 4 size (3.5 mm) needles, DPNs or long circular needles for magic loop

NOTIONS

Crochet hook, waste yarn, tapestry needle, stitch marker

GAUGE

23 stitches and 36 rows = 4 inches x 4 inches in stockinette stitch

Introduction

The color of this yarn makes me think of sea glass, delicate and frosted. I wanted the pattern to reflect those feelings so I added some light leaf details to the cuffs. These are perfect for picking up shells on the beach on a cold day.

PATTERN

These mitts are worked sideways and then grafted. Ribbing and thumb are picked up and worked in the round.

When instructed to hide wraps, pick up wrap and place it on the left needle, knit or purl the wrap together with the next st on the needle.

Both mitts are worked identically.

Provisional cast on

With the waste yarn and crochet hook, chain 40 (43, 46) sts. Using the working needles and main yarn, pick up and knit 1 st in each bump on the crochet chain. 40 (43, 46) sts

Row A (RS): p21 (24, 27), pm, p4, k1tbl, p8, k1tbl, p5.

Row B (WS): k5, p1tbl, k8, p1tbl, k4, sm, k to end.

Size M only

Work Rows A & B once more.

Size L only

Work Rows A & B two more times.

Leaf Chart (first repeat)

Work Rows 1-26 of Leaf Chart as follows:

RS rows: p to marker, sm, work chart.

WS rows: work chart, sm, p to end.

Size M only

Work Row A & B once more.

Size L only

Work Row A & B two more times.

Thumb Gusset

Row 1: p9 (10, 12), place the 9 (10, 12) sts just worked onto a stitch holder, p2, W&T.

Row 2: k to end

Row 3: p to wrapped stitch, hide wrap, p2, W&T.

Row 4: k to end

Repeat Rows 3 & 4 two (3, 3) more times.

Row 5: p to wrapped stitch, hide wrap, sm, p4, k1tbl, p8, k1tbl, p5.

Row 6: k5, p1tbl, k8, p1tbl, k4, sm, k to end.

Row 7: p to 1 st before marker, W&T.

Row 8: k3, pm, k to end.

Row 9: p to marker, rm, W&T.

Row 10: k3, pm, k to end.

Repeat Rows 9 & 10 two (3, 3) more times.

Row 11: p to marker, rm, p to next marker, sm, p4, k1tbl, p8, k1tbl, p5.

Row 12: k5, p1tbl, k8, p1tbl, k4, sm, k to end, place the 9 (9, 12) held sts from the stitch holder onto a needle, knit across them.

Size M only

Work Row A & B once more.

Size L only

Work Row A & B two more times.

Leaf Chart (second repeat)

Work Rows 1-26 of Leaf Chart as instructed in the first repeat.

Size M only

Work Row A & B once more.

Size L only

Work Row A & B two more times.

Grafting

Undo the crochet chain and place the 40 (43, 46) provisionally cast on sts onto another needle.

Using the Kitchener grafting technique, graft the both sets of sts together using the reverse stockinette grafting technique.
*Work in reverse stockinette grafting technique until 2 sts before the knit rib on the back needle and 1 st before the knit rib on the front needle.

Insert the tapestry needle front to back on the first st of the back needle and slip it off of the needle.
Insert the tapestry needle back to front in the next st on the back needle.

On the front needle, insert the tapestry needle back to front in the first st and then slip the st off of the needle.
Insert the tapestry needle front to back in the next st on front needle.

Insert the tapestry needle back to front on the first st of the back needle and then slip the st off of the needle.
Insert the tapestry needle from front to back in the next st on the back needle.

On the front needle, insert the tapestry needle front to back in the first st and then slip the st off of the needle.
Insert the tapestry needle front to back in the next st on front needle.

Repeat from * once more.

Continue in reverse stockinette graft to end.

Wrist Ribbing

Working across the bottom of the mitts, pick up and k 38 (44, 48) sts, pm and join in the round. To distribute sts evenly, pick up 2 sts every three rows.

Next round: (k1, p1) around.
Repeat previous round seven more times.
Bind off all sts in pattern.

Top Ribbing

Work same as Wrist ribbing, picking up sts along the top of the mitts.

Thumb

Starting in the crook of the thumb, pick up and k 1 st, pick up and k 12 (16, 16) sts around the thumb opening, pick up one final stitch in the crook of the thumb, pm and join in the round. 14 (18, 18) sts

Round 1: k2tog, (p1, k1) to last 2 sts remain, ssp. 12 (16, 16) sts.

Next round: (k1, p1) around.
Repeat previous round six more times.
Bind off all sts in pattern.

Finishing

Weave in all ends and block to finished measurements.

Leaf Chart

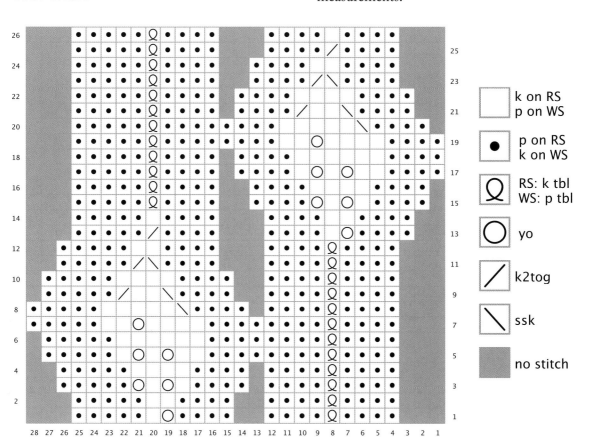

☐	k on RS / p on WS
•	p on RS / k on WS
℧	RS: k tbl / WS: p tbl
○	yo
╱	k2tog
╲	ssk
▨	no stitch

Projects #13 & 14

WINHALL

Cross-stitch Hat & Mittens

DETAILS

YARN

Wonderland Yarns Mad Hatter
(100% superwash merino wool, 113g, 344yds/314m)
MC: Color 34 Dormouse, 2 skeins
CC: Color 15 Muchness, 1 skein

FINISHED MEASUREMENTS

Hat:
S (M, L)
Circumference: 16 (18, 20) inches at brim, unstretched.
While choosing a size, keep in mind that brim will stretch 1-2 inches

Mittens:
S (M, L)
Hand circumference: 6.5 (7.5, 8.5) inches
Cuff to finger tip: 9.8 (10.3, 10.8) inches

Both samples shown in M

RECOMMENDED NEEDLES

US 4 size (3.5 mm) needles, 16-inch circular and DPNs, or long circular
needles for magic loop

NOTIONS

Tapestry needle, stitch marker, stitch holders

GAUGE

23 stitches and 36 rounds = 4 inches x 4 inches in stockinette stitch

Introduction

The inspiration for these pieces stems from trips to flea markets, where I love to pick up hand-stitched vintage linens. When I first saw these two yarns next to each other, I knew they belonged together. I love how the rich brown tones in the main yarn set off the blue accents.

PATTERNS

Main Stitch Pattern

(worked in the round, over a multiple of 4 sts):

Rounds 1-2: k all sts around.

Round 3: (k2, p2) around.

Rounds 4-6: Repeat rounds 1-3.

Round 7-8: k all sts around.

Round 9: (p2, k2) around.

Rounds 10-12: Repeat rounds 7-9.

Hat

With MC yarn, cast on 92 (104, 116) sts, place marker, and join in the round.

Next round: (k1, p1) around.
Work previous round 11 more times.

Increase round: *k4, M1, repeat from * to last 12 (8, 4) sts, knit to end. 112 (128, 144) sts

Work rounds 1-12 of Main Stitch Pattern five times, for a total of 60 rounds.

Decrease Rounds

Round 1-2: k all sts around.

Round 3: *k2, p2, k2, k2tog, repeat from * to end. 98 (112, 126) sts

Round 4: k all sts around.

Round 5: *k5, k2tog, repeat from * to end. 84 (96, 108) sts

Round 6: (k2, p2, k2) around.

Round 7: *k4, k2tog, repeat from * to end. 70 (80, 90) sts

Round 8: k all sts around.

Round 9: *p2, k1, k2tog, repeat from * to end. 56 (64, 72) sts

Round 10: k all sts around.

Round 11: *k2, k2tog, repeat from * to end. 42 (48, 54) sts

Round 12: *p2, k1, repeat from * to end.

Round 13: *k1, k2tog, repeat from * to end. 28 (32, 36) sts

Round 14: k all sts around.

Round 15: *k2tog, repeat from * to end. 14 (16, 18) sts

Round 16: *k2tog, repeat from * to end. 7 (8, 9) sts

Break yarn and pull through the remaining sts and secure.

Mittens

Both mittens are worked identically.

With MC yarn, cast on 30 (38, 42) sts, place marker, and join in the round.

Next round: (k1, p1) around.
Work previous round 17 more times.

Set-up round: *k5 (6, 7), M1, repeat from * until - (2, -) sts remain, k - (2, -). 36 (44, 48) sts
Work Rounds 1-12 of Main Stitch Pattern once.

Thumb Gusset

Round 13: k to last 2 sts, pm, M1R, k2, M1L. 4 sts after marker

Round 14: k all sts around.

Round 15: (k2, p2) to 2 sts before marker, k2, sm, k1, p2, k1.

Round 16: k to marker, sm, M1R, k to last st, M1L. 2 sts increased

Round 17: k all sts around.

Round 18: (k2, p2) to 2 sts before marker, k2, sm, k2, p2, k2.

Round 19: Same as Round 16.

Round 20: k all sts around.

Round 21: (p2, k2) to 2 sts before marker, k2, sm, k1, p2, k2, p2, k1.

Round 22: Repeat Round 16.

Round 23: k all sts around.

Round 24: (p2, k2) to 2 sts before marker, k2, sm, (k2, p2) twice, k2

Round 25: Repeat Round 16.

Round 26: k all sts around.

Round 27: (k2, p2) to 2 sts before marker, k2, sm, k1, (p2, k2) twice, p2, k1.

Round 28: Repeat Round 16. 14 sts after marker, 48 (56, 60) sts total.

Round 29: k all sts around.

Size S only

Skip to Hand section.

Sizes M and L only

Round 30: (k2, p2) to 2 sts before marker, k2, sm, (k2, p2) three times, k2.

Round 31: Same as Round 16. 16 sts after marker, - (58, 62) sts total.

Round 32: k all sts around.

Size M only

Skip to Hand section.

Size L only

Round 33: (p2, k2) to 2 sts before marker, k2, sm, k1, (p2, k2) three times, p2, k1.

Round 34: k to marker, sm, M1R, k16, M1L. 18 sts after marker, - (-, 64) sts total

Round 35: k all sts around.

Hand
Size S only

Round 30: (k2, p2) to 2 sts before marker, k2, rm, place the 14 sts after the marker onto a stitch holder, cast on 4 sts. 38 sts

Round 31: slip the last stitch cast on from the previous round to the beginning of this round, k2tog, k to last 4 sts, ssk, k2. 36 sts

Round 32-36: Work rounds 8-12 of Main Stitch Pattern.

Rounds 37-64: Work rounds 1-12 of Main Stitch Pattern twice, then work rounds 1-4 once more.

Round 65: *k2, k2tog, repeat from * to end. 27 sts

Rounds 66-67: k all sts around.

Round 68: *k1, k2tog, repeat from * to end. 18 sts

Round 69: *k2tog, repeat from * to end. 9 sts

Round 70: *k2tog, repeat from * to last st, k1. 5 sts

Break yarn and pull through the remaining stitches. Tighten to close the hole and secure.

Size M only

Round 33: (p2, k2) to 2 sts before marker, k2, rm, place the 16 sts after the marker onto a stitch holder, cast on 4 sts. 46 sts

Round 34: slip the last stitch cast on from the previous round to the beginning of this round, k2tog, k to last 4 sts remain, ssk, k2. 44 sts

Round 35: Work rounds 11-12 of Main Stitch Pattern.

Round 36: *p2, k2, repeat from * to end

Rounds 37-68: Work rounds 1-12 of Main Stitch Pattern twice, then work rounds 1-8 once more.

Round 69: *k2, k2tog, repeat from * to end. 33 sts

Rounds 70-72: k all sts around.

Round 71: *k1, k2tog, repeat from * to end. 22 sts

Round 73: *k2tog, repeat from * to end. 11 sts

Round 74: *k2tog, repeat from * to last st, k1. 6 sts

Break yarn and pull through the remaining stitches. Tighten to close the hole and secure.

Size L only

Round 36: (p2, k2) to 2 sts before marker, k2, rm, place the 18 sts after the marker onto a stitch holder, cast on 4 sts. 50 sts

Round 37: slip the last stitch cast on from the previous round to the beginning of this round, k2tog, k to last 4 sts, ssk, k2. 48 sts

Rounds 38-48: Work rounds 2-12 of Main Stitch Pattern.

Rounds 49-72: Work rounds 1-12 of Main Stitch Pattern twice.

Round 73: *k2, k2tog, repeat from * to end. 36 sts

Rounds 74: k all sts around.

Round 75: *k1, k2tog, repeat from * to end. 24 sts

Round 76: k all sts around.

Round 77: *k2tog, repeat from * to end. 12 sts

Round 78: *k2tog, repeat from * to end. 6 sts
Break yarn and pull through the remaining stitches. Tighten to close the hole and secure.

Thumb

Return the 14 (16, 18) thumb sts to the needles. With RS facing, rejoin yarn and pick up and knit 2 sts in the crook of the thumb, over the cast on stitches. Arrange the sts so that the first picked up st becomes the last st of the round and the second picked up st becomes to first st of the round. 16 (18, 20) sts.

Size S only

Round 1: sl1, (k2, p2) to last 3 sts, k1, ssk. 15 sts

Round 2: k2tog, k to end. 14 sts

Round 3: k all sts around.

Round 4: (p2, k2) to last 2 sts, p2.

Rounds 5-6: k all sts around.

Round 7-9: Repeat rounds 4-6.

Round 10: (k2, p2) to last 2 sts, k2.

Rounds 11-12: k all sts around.

Rounds 13-15: Repeat rounds 10-12.

Round 16: Repeat round 4.

Rounds 17-18: k all sts around.

Rounds 19: Repeat round 4.

Round 20: k2tog around. 7 sts

Round 21: k all sts around.

Round 22: k2tog to last st, k1. 4 sts

Break yarn and pull through the remaining stitches. Tighten to close the hole and secure.

Size M only

Round 1: sl1, k1, (p2, k2) to last 4 sts, p2, ssk. 17 sts

Round 2: k2tog, k to end. 16 sts

Rounds 3-4: Work rounds 11-12 of Main Stitch Pattern.

Round 5-20: Work rounds 1-12 of Main Stitch Pattern once, then work rounds 1-4 once more.

Round 21: k2tog to end. 8 sts

Round 22: k all sts around.

Round 23: k2tog to end. 4 sts

Break yarn and pull through the remaining stitches. Tighten to close the hole and secure.

Size L only

Round 1: sl1, (k2, p2) to last 3 sts, k1, ssk. 19 sts

Round 2: k2tog, k to end. 18 sts

Round 3: k all sts around.

Round 4: (k2, p2) to last 2 sts, k2.

Rounds 5-6: k all sts around.

Round 7: Repeat round 4.

Rounds 8-9: k all sts around.

Round 10: (p2, k2) to last 2 sts, p2.

Rounds 11-13: Repeat rounds 8-10.

Rounds 14-15: k all sts around.

Round 16: Repeat round 4.

Rounds 17-19: repeat rounds 14-16.

Rounds 20-22: k all sts around.

Round 23: k2tog to end. 9 sts

Round 24: k all sts around.

Round 25: k2tog to last st, k1. 5 sts

Break yarn and pull through the remaining stitches. Tighten to close the hole and secure.

Finishing

Weave in all ends. Work cross stitch instructions.

CROSS STITCH

Cut a 72-inch length of CC yarn (join additional lengths of yarn as needed). Thread the yarn through the tapestry needle and pull it so that the ends of the yarn are even. You will be using two strands of yarn for each embroidery stitch.

The cross stitches on the hat and mittens will be worked very much like a cross stitch on canvas. The (k2, p2) pattern knit into the fabric creates "squares" over which the cross stitches will be made. Choose a row of squares to begin working the cross stitches.

Top to Bottom Cross

*Starting from the inside of the item, inserted the tapestry needle next to the top left purl stitch (1a) of one square. Next insert the tapestry needle next to the bottom right purl stitch (1b) of the square and pull through. Make sure to keep the stitches loose so that they can stretch with the item. Repeat from * in the square to the right of the one just worked (2a and 2b). Continue in this manner until all squares in the row have been worked.

Bottom to Top Cross

*Starting from the inside of the item, inserted the tapestry needle next to the bottom left purl stitch (1c) of one square. Next insert the tapestry needle next to the top right purl stitch (1d) of the square and pull through. Repeat from * in the square to the right of the one just worked (2c and 2d). Continue in this manner until all squares in the row have been worked.

Continue working Top to Bottom Cross and Bottom to Top Cross stitches until all rows on the item have been stitched. Secure ends and block item.

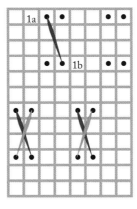
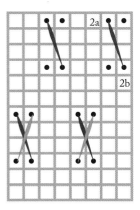
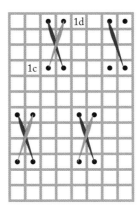
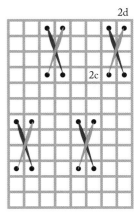

American Yarn File #11

SPINCYCLE YARNS

Bellingham, Washington

What led you to your current path?

Kate and I (Rachel) met by chance eleven years ago when we were working at our local food coop. We were both knitting and dyeing and handspinning, and we were instantly friend-crushing on each other. She had gotten into all of the above much earlier; her parents were hippy homesteaders in the 80's and there was a spinning wheel in her living room for all of her early childhood. As for me, I found my way to knitting and spinning during the six months I spent tree-sitting in Northern California. I had a drop spindle and some awful greasy mohair and one pair of straight 10.5's. And I made the most of it!

When we formed a business and started selling our handspun yarns at the farmers' market ten years ago, we never dreamed it would evolve into yarn production on this scale! It makes me wonder what the next ten years will bring!

We love our jobs so much! The work is creative and productive and we get to meet so many other amazing yarn producers, as well as designers. I can't imagine doing anything else and being as happy doing it. I love long days in the dye house as much as I love photographing yarns and tweaking our website. And now that we've moved to using only USA-grown wool, we both feel even more connected to our process because we know so many of the other people involved!

We started out as a handspinnery, and even now that most of our yarns are spun at our mill, we approach the process as handspinners so that our yarns would still have that same look and feel.

All of our yarns are dyed in the wool, so color shifts are long, gradual, and unpredictable. Every skein is different, even from the same dyelot. All the hues of the colorway will be there, but the order in which they repeat, the lengths of the repeats, even the in-between colors that happen in the blending are all one-of-a-kind. And especially with a 2-ply yarn like Dyed In The Wool or Knit Fast, Die Young, the possibilities of combinations are endless. Our process is not the easiest way to dye yarns! But we stick to it because the yarns we produce are so unlike everything else out there.

Project #15

LUMMI

Bias Brioche

DETAILS

YARN

Spincycle Yarns Knit Fast, Die Young
(100% American wool, 100 yds/91 m)
Color Brass Monkey, 1 skein

FINISHED MEASUREMENTS

8 inches wide x 29 inches in circumference

RECOMMENDED NEEDLES

US size 15 (10.00 mm) needles

NOTIONS

Waste yarn, tapestry needle, stitch marker, crochet hook

GAUGE

8 stitches and 18 rows = 4 inches x 4 inches in (k1B, p1) ribbing pattern
(Gauge is not critical for this project but will affect yardage)

Introduction

The name of this yarn says it all—Knit Fast Die Young. Indeed, the thickness of the yarn makes for a quick knit. The colors remind me of the different stria evident in sandstone rock formations of the American Southwest.

PATTERN

With the waste yarn and crochet hook, chain 20 sts. Using working needles and main yarn, pick up and knit 1 st in each bump on the crochet chain. 20 sts

Set-up Row
k2, (k1, p1) to last 2 sts, k2.

Row 1 (RS): k2, yo, (k1B, p1) to last 2 sts, k2. 21 sts

Row 2 (WS): k1, k2tog, k to last 3 sts remain, k1tbl, k2. 20 sts

Row 3: k2, yo, (p1, k1B) to last 2 sts, k2. 21 sts

Row 4: k1, k2tog, k to last 3 sts, p1tbl, k2. 20 sts

Repeat rows 1-4 nineteen more times, or to desired length.

Grafting

Using the Kitchener grafting technique, work the first two sts on both needles using the garter stitch graft, work the next 16 sts on both needles using the (k1, p1) graft, work the remaining 2 sts on both needles using the garter stitch graft.

Finishing

Weave in all ends and block.

American Yarn File #12

LAKES YARN AND FIBER

Coeur d'Alene, Idaho

Ami Volz

What led you to your current path?

My first introduction to knitting (and hence wool) was as a child watching my grandmother knit. It fascinated me enough that I decided to learn, and I spent my high school years knitting giant hats and too-small socks. I remember being obsessed with Nancy Bush's Folk Socks and planning on knitting every pair—so far I've only knit three pairs from that book, but I still dream of working my way through it. After being introduced to the world of Internet knitting through knitting blogs I became even more fascinated with the entire process of wool—from raising sheep to cleaning the wool to spinning and dyeing. Despite years of pestering, I was never able to wheedle my husband into buying me a sheep ranch, however, I did persuade my dad to help me raise a very small handspinning flock on his plot of land in 2012. We started with 3 Finnsheep and this year we had as many as 18 at once.

Dyeing was a sideline to my total fascination with wool. It grew out of my curiosity about every aspect of yarn prep and was nurtured by a friend into a full-blown obsession. I spent about 12 months dyeing over 1000 samples just so that I could teach myself how to mix colors from primaries. I don't have any artistic background at all—my trade is as a Registered Nurse (I still work as an RN), but I love to read and I spent many hours poring over dyeing books, Internet forums and Youtube tutorials about dyeing. My plan was never to open a yarn dyeing business, but I love to create color and I have to do something with all of the excess.

What keeps you on this path?

I really and truly just enjoy dyeing yarn. I see things around me... honeysuckle blossoms, the color of the lake at dawn, a cloudy sky and have the desire to translate those colors onto yarn. I love to turn off my phone, put on headphones and crank music while I splash about in my dye pots. I very much enjoy the solitary nature of my work and being unplugged from the world.

I also love seeing what people make out of my yarn and the Internet enables me to see those finished projects. I am constantly amazed and grateful that people choose my yarn for their projects.

Raising sheep has been an absolute joy and a huge learning process. I wish we could do it on a larger scale, but we are limited by the amount of land my family has. All of the sheep have their own personality and preferences. Because we are small we can spend a lot of time with them, much like people do with their dogs and cats. During the warmer months we even take our lawn chairs out into the field to sit with the sheep and keep them company. We are learning about fleece management—what kind of minerals we feed make a big difference in the quality of the fleece—who knew? There is just so much to learn and see in our small-scale operation.

Project #16

COEUR D'ALENE

Ladies Sweater

DETAILS

YARN

Lakes Yarn & Fiber Targhee Worsted
(100% targhee wool, 120 g, 310 yds /283 m)
Color Mustache Man, 4 (4, 5, 5, 6, 6, 7, 7, 8) skeins
This is a limited edition yarn. Lakes Yarn & Fiber Lochsa DK would make an excellent substitute.

FINISHED MEASUREMENTS

XS (S, M, L, XL, 2X, 3X, 4X, 5X)
Bust circumference: 31 (35.5, 39.5, 43, 47, 51, 55, 59, 63) inches
To fit bust: 30 (34, 38, 42, 46, 49, 54, 58, 62) inches with 1-2" positive ease
Sample shown in Size S

RECOMMENDED NEEDLES

US size 8 (5.0mm) needles, 32-inch circular and DPNs, or long circular needles for magic loop

NOTIONS

Tapestry needle, stitch markers, 2 stitch holders or waste yarn

GAUGE

18 stitches and 24 rounds = 4 inches x 4 inches in stockinette stitch

Introduction

The earthy color reminds me of nights in log cabins—two fingers of bourbon, hot embers glowing in the fireplace, and the silent forest outside. The natural qualities of Targhee wool really help the slip-stitch design on the yoke of this sweater stand out.

PATTERN

Neck

Cast on 80 (96, 104, 104, 112, 112, 112, 120, 128) sts, pm, and join in the round.

Rounds 1: (k2, p2) around.

Round 2: Same as Round 1.

Round 3: (k2, p2) 5 (6, 6, 6, 7, 7, 7, 7, 8) times, M1, pm, k2, M1, p2, (k2, p2) 9 (11, 12, 12, 13, 13, 13, 14, 15) times, M1, pm, k2, M1, p2, (k2, p2) 4 (5, 6, 6, 6, 6, 6, 7, 7) times. 4 sts increased

Round 4: *(k2, p2) to 1 st before marker, k1, sm, k3, p2, repeat from * once more, (k2, p2) to end.

Round 5: *(k2, p2) to 1 st before marker, k1, M1, sm, k2, M1, k1, p2, repeat from * once more, (k2, p2) to end. 4 sts increased

Round 6: *(k2, p2) to 2 sts before marker, k2, sm, k2, repeat from * once more, (k2, p2) to end.

Round 7: *(k2, p2) to 2 sts before marker, k2, M1p, sm, k2, M1p, repeat from * once more, (k2, p2) to end. 4 sts increased

Round 8: *(k2, p2) to 3 sts before marker, k2, p1, sm, k2, p1, repeat from * once more, (k2, p2) to end.

Round 9: *(k2, p2) to 3 sts before marker, k2, p1, M1p, rm, k2, M1p, p1, repeat from * once more, (k2, p2) to end. 4 sts increased

Round 10: (k2, p2) to end.

96 (112, 120, 120, 128, 128, 128, 136, 144) sts

Yoke
Setup round:
Sizes XS: (p24, M1p) 4 times.
Size S: (p14, M1p) 8 times.
Size M: (p12, M1p) 10 times.
Size L: (p6, M1p) 20 times.
Sizes XL: (p10, M1p) 12 times, p8.
Sizes 2X and 3X: (p5, M1p) 22 times, p18.
Sizes 4X: (p5, M1p) 24 times, p16.
Sizes 5X: (p24, M1p) 6 times.
100 (120, 130, 140, 140, 150, 150, 160, 150) sts

Forest Yoke Charts

Select the appropriate Forest Yoke chart for your size. Beginning on Round 1, work through all rounds of the chart. On each round, the charted pattern will be repeated 10 (12, 13, 14, 14, 15, 15, 16, 15) times.

After working the last row of the chart, you will have 180 (216, 234, 252, 280, 300, 330, 352, 360) sts.

Sleeve Separation Round:

Work in (k1, p1) pattern as established for 29 (36, 39, 42, 46, 48, 53, 56, 59) sts, slip the next 34 (38, 41, 44, 50, 56, 62, 66, 65) sts onto a stitch holder, cast on 14 (10, 13, 14, 16, 20, 20, 22, 27) sts, work in (k1, p1) pattern as established for 56 (70, 76,

82, 90, 94, 103, 110, 115) sts, slip the next 34 (38, 41, 44, 50, 56, 62, 66, 65) sts onto a stitch holder, cast on 14 (10, 13, 14, 16, 20, 20, 22, 27) sts, work in (k1, p1) pattern as established until the end of the round. 140 (160, 178, 192, 212, 228, 246, 264, 284) sts

Work 12 rounds in (k1, p1) ribbing as established.

Work 6 (10, 10, 11, 14, 15, 15, 18, 17) rounds in stockinette stitch.

Bust Decreases

Round 1: k 35 (40, 45, 49, 53, 57, 62, 66, 72) sts, pm, ssk, k 66 (76, 84, 92, 102, 110, 118, 128, 136), k2tog, pm, k to end. 2 sts decreased

Work 1 (1, 1, 2, 1, 1, 1, 1, 1) round(s) in stockinette stitch (knit each round).

Decrease Round: k to marker, sm, ssk, k to 2 sts before marker, k2tog, sm, k to end. 2 sts decreased

Continuing in stockinette stitch, repeat Decrease Round every 2 (2, 2, 3, 2, 2, 2, 2, 2) rounds, 12 (12, 13, 8, 12, 12, 12, 12, 12) more times. 112 (132, 148, 172, 184, 200, 218, 236, 256) sts

Work 2 (4, 2, 9, 8, 4, 1, 12, 13) rounds in stockinette stitch.

Hip Increases

Increase Round: k to marker, sm, k1, LLI, k to 1 st before marker, RLI, k1, sm, k to end. 2 sts increased

Continuing in stockinette stitch, repeat Increase Round every 2 (2, 2, 3, 2, 2, 2, 2, 2) rounds, 13 (15, 15, 9, 13, 19, 14, 13, 13) more times. 140 (164, 180, 192, 212, 240, 248, 264, 284) sts

Work 2 (2, 2, 3, 2, 2, 2, 2, 2) rounds in stockinette stitch.

Short Row Hem

This section will be worked back and forth, in short rows.

Row 1 (RS): k to first marker, sm, k 17 (21, 22, 24, 26, 31, 31, 33, 35), w&t.

Row 2 (WS): sl1, *p to marker, sm, p to marker, rm, p to marker, sm, p 17 (21, 22, 24, 26, 31, 31, 33, 35), w&t.

Row 3: sl1, k to 3 sts before previous wrap, w&t.

Row 4: sl1, p to 3 sts before previous wrap, w&t.

Repeat Rows 3 and 4 two more times.

Next row (RS): sl1, k to end, picking up wraps as you come to them.

From here begin knitting in the round again.

Next round: (k2, p2) around.

Repeat previous round 11 more times.

Loosely bind off all sts in pattern.

Sleeves

Left sleeve

Pick up and knit 14 (10, 13, 14, 16, 20, 20, 22, 27) sts from the underarm cast on edge, place the 34 (38, 41, 44, 50, 56, 62, 66, 65) sts from the stitch holder on to a needle and work across them in (k1, p1) pattern as established, pm, and join in the round.
48 (48, 54, 58, 66, 76, 82, 88, 92) sts

Next round: (k2, p2) around.
Repeat previous round 11 more times.

Work 45 (48, 30, 18, 22, 26, 14, 8, 9) rounds in stockinette stitch.

Sleeve decreases
Decrease Round: k2tog, k to last 2 sts, ssk. 2 sts decreased.

Continuing in stockinette stitch, repeat Decrease Round every 6 (6, 6, 6, 6, 4, 4, 4, 4) rounds, 5 (5, 8, 8, 10, 15, 18, 20, 20) more times.
36 (36, 36, 40, 44, 44, 48, 48, 48) sts

Work 6 (6, 6, 6, 6, 4, 4, 4, 4) rounds in stockinette stitch.

Cuff

Next round: (k2, p2) around.
Repeat previous round 11 more times.
Loosely bind off all sts in pattern.

Right Sleeve

Place the 34 (38, 41, 44, 50, 56, 62, 66, 65) sts from the stitch holder on to a needle and knit all sts from the needle in k1, p1 pattern as established, pick up and knit 14 (10, 13, 14, 16, 20, 20, 22, 27) sts from the underarm cast on edge, pm and join in the round.
48 (48, 54, 58, 66, 76, 82, 88, 92) sts

Work the remainder of the sleeve same as left sleeve.

Finishing
Weave in all ends and block according to the schematic.

Sizes XS, S, M, L

Sizes XL, 2X

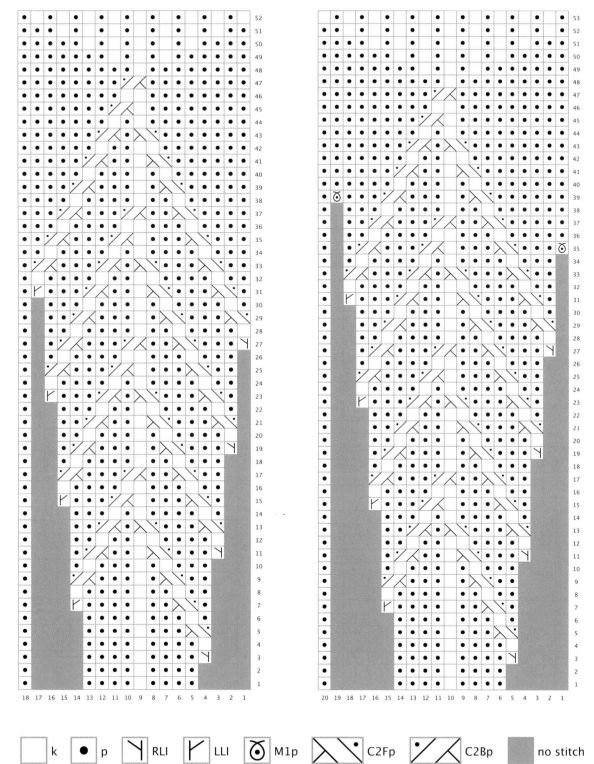

	k	●	p	⅄	RLI	Ⅴ	LLI	⊙	M1p	⤬	⟍•	C2Fp	⟋• ⟋	C2Bp		no stitch

105

Sizes 3X, 4X

Size 5X

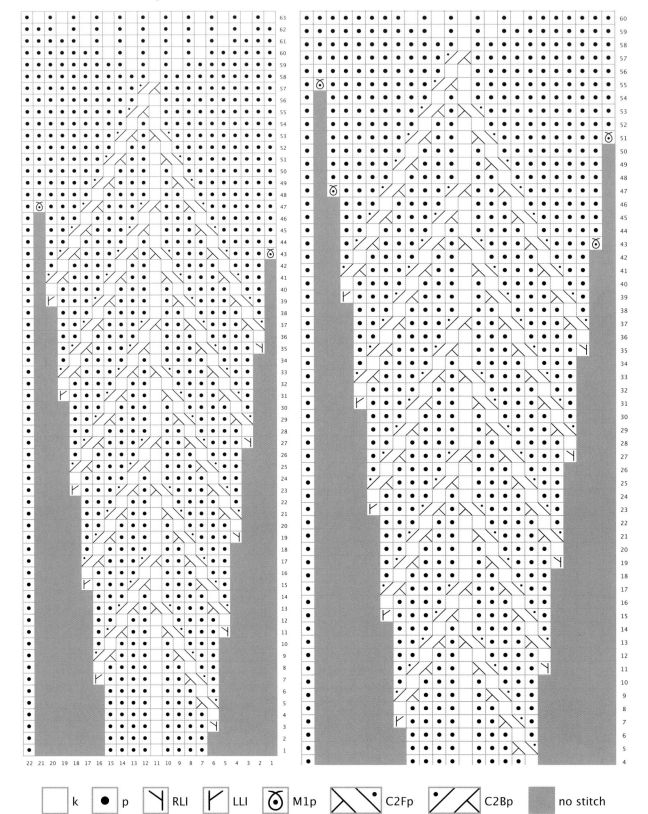

k □ **p** ● **RLI** ⅄ **LLI** ⅄ **M1p** ⌀ **C2Fp** ╲•╱ **C2Bp** •╱╲ **no stitch** ▨

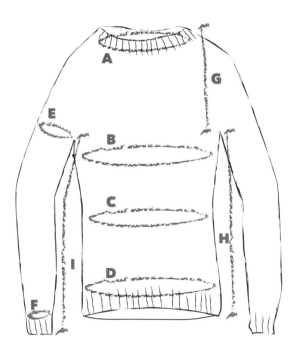

A: 17.75 (21.25, 23, 23, 25, 25, 25, 26.75, 28.5) inches

B: 31 (35.5, 39.5, 43, 47, 51, 55, 59, 63) inches

C: 25 (29, 33, 39, 41, 44, 49, 53, 57) inches

D: 31 (36, 39, 43, 47, 53, 55, 58.6, 63) inches

E: 10.75 (10.75, 12, 13, 14.75, 17, 18.25, 19.5, 20.5) inches

F: 8 (8, 8, 8.75, 9.75, 9.75, 10.5, 10.5, 10.5) inches

G: 10.5 (10.5, 10.5, 10.5, 10.75, 10.75, 12.25, 12.25, 12.5) inches

H: 14 (14, 15, 15, 15, 15.5, 15.5, 16, 16) inches

I: 17.5 (18, 18, 18.5, 18.5, 19, 19, 19.5, 19.5) inches

American Yarn File #13

PIGEON ROOF STUDIOS

Emeryville, California

Krista McCurdy

What led you to your current path?

I stumbled into it, really. I had knit off and on all my life, mainly endless scarves in acrylic yarn, but when I picked up knitting again after college, I started working with better yarn and discovered blogs. People had started experimenting with Kool-Aid dyeing on blogs, and I saw that and thought, "that looks like fun. I can do that." I'd actually done a little bit of dyeing in a textile class I'd taken in college, and still had a vague recollection of it. Anyways, I started dyeing with Kool-Aid, and then somehow—I still can't remember exactly how—I decided to start playing around with acid dyes. I pretty much taught myself all my processes; other than reading the basics of using heat and acid (vinegar or citric acid), it's been one big experiment! It all spiraled from there. One thing led to another, and I found myself doing this full time! I've always liked working for myself, so it was a pretty natural progression.

What keeps you on this path?

I like making things—it's really as simple as that! That said, there's always so much more to learn. I've been doing this now for eight years, and I keep learning new things and ways to do things constantly. Refining some techniques, discarding some, finding new ones. I love working with color. I've recently started doing some natural dyeing, and that's really exciting me because it's a whole different ballgame than working with acid dyes—there's so much new stuff to learn.

What would you like people to know about your process?

I suppose that one thing would be that my process is endlessly developing, endlessly changing. I'm constantly experimenting—I'm not a very good production dyer, because I love making new things, coming up with new colors. I suppose also, that I am a one-woman show working out of a very small studio! I have a friend that has been helping me one day a week, but other than that, it's just me. In the end, being able to work for myself, and to make beautiful things on a daily basis is pretty amazing.

Project #17

Annadel

Leg Warmers

DETAILS

YARN

Pigeonroof Studios Squishy DK
(100% superwash merino wool, 113g, 300 yds/274 m)
Color Pichouline, 2 skeins

FINISHED MEASUREMENTS

M (L)
Calf circumference: 14 (15) inches
Foot circumference: 8 (9) inches
Length: 21.4 (21.4) inches
Choose a size based on your foot circumference
Sample shown in M

RECOMMENDED NEEDLES

US size 4 (3.5 mm) and US size 6 (4 mm) needles, DPNs or long circular needles for magic loop

NOTIONS

Waste yarn, tapestry needle, stitch marker

GAUGE

22.5 stitches and 34 rounds = 4 inches x 4 inches in (k1, p1) ribbing with smaller needles
17.5 stitches and 36 rounds = 4 inches x 4 inches in (k1B, p1) ribbing with larger needles

Introduction

The colors coming out of Pigeon Roof Studios are vivid and complex. When knit, the tonal variation over the strand of yarn adds a great deal of depth to the finished garment—these leg warmers are long and broad enough to really show off the different tones.

PATTERN

Both leg warmers are worked identically, from the bottom up.

With smaller needles, cast on 46 (50) sts, place marker, and join in the round.

Next round: (k1, p1) around.
Repeat previous round 24 more times.

Heel

Using waste yarn, k23 (25) sts. Return the 23 (25) sts just knit to the left hand needle. You will work these sts in pattern on the next round.

Continuing with your main yarn,
work 12 rounds in (k1, p1) ribbing.

Switch to larger needles.
Work 2 rounds in (k1, p1) ribbing.

Brioche Ribbing

Round 1: (k1B, p1) around.

Size L : Skip to round 20.

Size M only:
Round 2: p11, 1into3p, p to end. 48 sts
Round 3: (k1B, p1) 6 times, k1, p1, (k1B, p1) to end.
Round 4: p all sts around.
Round 5: (k1B, p1) around.
Rounds 6-19: Work rows 4-5 seven more times.

Both Sizes
Round 20: p12, 1into3, p to end. 50 (52) sts
Round 21: (k1B, p1) 6 times, (k1, p1) twice, (k1B, p1) to end.
Rounds 22-37: Work rounds 4-5 eight times.

Round 38: p13, 1into3p, p to end. 52 (54) sts
Round 39: (k1B, p1) 7 times, k1, p1, (k1B, p1) to end.
Rounds 40-55: Work rounds 4-5 eight times.

Round 56: p14, 1into3, p to end. 54 (56) sts
Round 57: (k1B, p1) 7 times, (k1, p1) twice, (k1B, p1) to end.
Rounds 58-73: Work rounds 4-5 eight times.

Round 74: p15, 1into3p, p to end. 56 (58) sts
Round 75: (k1B, p1) 8 times, k1, p1, (k1B, p1) to end.
Rounds 76-91: Work rounds 4-5 eight times.

Round 92: p16, 1into3, p to end. 58 (60) sts
Round 93: (k1B, p1) 8 times, (k1, p1) twice, (k1B, p1) to end.
Rounds 94-109: Work rounds 4-5 eight times.
Round 110: p17, 1into3p, p to end. 60 (62) sts
Round 111: (k1B, p1) 9 times, k1, p1, (k1B, p1) to end.
Rounds 112-127: Work rounds 4-5 eight times.

Round 128: p18, 1into3, p to end. 62 (64) sts

Round 129: (k1B, p1) 9 times, (k1, p1) twice, (k1B, p1) to end.

Rounds 130-145: Work rounds 4-5 eight times.

Size M

Skip to Cuff.

Size L only

Round 146: p19, 1into3P, p to end. 66 sts

Round 147: (k1B, p1) 10 times, k1, p1, (k1B, p1) to end.

Rounds 148-163: Work rounds 4-5 eight times.

Cuff

Switch to smaller needles.

Next round: (k1, p1) around.

Repeat previous round 8 more times.

Bind off all sts in pattern.

Heel Opening

Remove the waste yarn and place live sts on either side of the waste yarn onto smaller needles. 46 (50) sts.

Attach yarn and bind off all sts in pattern. Make sure to use a stretchy bind off such as a sewn bind off.

Finishing

Weave in all ends and block.

Project #18

UMPQUA

Hat

DETAILS

YARN

Pigeon Roof Studios American Sock Mini Skein Set
(100% superwash merino wool, 240 yds/219 m {40 yds/ 36 m per mini skein})
Color Denim, 1 (1, 2) sets

FINISHED MEASUREMENTS

S (M, L)
Circumference: 16 (18, 20) inches at brim, unstretched
While choosing a size, keep in mind that brim will stretch 1-2"
Sample shown in M

RECOMMENDED NEEDLES

US size 3 (3.25 mm) needles, 16-inch circular and DPNs or long circular
needles for magic loop

NOTIONS

Tapestry needle, stitch marker

GAUGE

25 stitches and 34 rounds = 4 inches x 4 inches in stockinette stitch

Introduction

*The hanks of yarn in this mini skein kit seamlessly blend into one
another when knit, forming a lovely ombre. I designed this pattern to
play with the transitioning colors, like the darkening of the sea as the
shore gives way to deeper waters.*

PATTERN

Notes: Colors will be numbered from lightest to darkest as C1, C2, C3, C4, C5, C6.

Since the color progression section of the pattern calls for changing colors every round, the yarn will be carried up the back on the inside of the hat. To do this, the two resting colors (or the colors not used during the next round) will be wrapped over the working color (the color used in the next round). This will create a braid or twist of yarn at the point where the colors are changed. When carrying colors up the back, make sure to leave enough slack between rounds. If the yarn is pulled too tightly, it will distort the last stitch in created with that color.

With C6, cast on 100 (112, 124) sts, place marker, and join in the round.

Next round: (k1, p1) around.
Repeat previous round seven more times.

Color Progression
Round 1 (C6): k all sts around.
Round 2 (C5): k all sts around.
Round 3 (C4): k all sts around.
Repeat rounds 1-3 four more times.

Round 4 (C5): k all sts around.
Round 5 (C4): k all sts around.
Round 6 (C3): k all sts around.
Repeat rounds 4-6 four more times.

Round 7 (C4): k all sts around.
Round 8 (C3): k all sts around.
Round 9 (C2): k all sts around.
Repeat rounds 7-9 four more times.

Round 10 (C3): k all sts around.
Round 11 (C2): k all sts around
Round 12 (C1): k all sts around.
Repeat rounds 10-12 four more times.

Decrease Rounds: Continue working in C1 only for the remainder of the hat.

Round 1: (k2tog, k2) to end. 75 (84, 93) sts
Rounds 2, 4, 6, 8: k all sts around.
Round 3: (k2tog, k1) to end. 50 (56, 62) sts
Round 5: k2tog to end. 25 (28, 31) sts.
Round 7: k1 (0, 1), k2tog to end. 13 (14, 16) sts.
Round 9: k1 (0, 0), k2tog to end. 7 (7, 8) sts.

Break yarn and pull through remaining sts.

Finishing
Weave in all ends and block.

American Yarn File #14

JILL DRAPER MAKES STUFF

Hudson Valley, New York

Jill Draper

What led you to your current path?

I studied Fashion Design at Pratt Institute because I loved making things, specifically clothing but I have always dabbled in a bit of everything. After working in the commercial fashion industry for a bit I realized I was touching nothing but pencils with my hands. I wanted to be producing something with my own hands besides sketches to be sent off and made elsewhere. Jill Draper Makes Stuff started out as handspun yarn made from roving I had dyed among other decorative items. The yarn was what sold best at craft fairs & I eventually couldn't keep up with the demand. I started hand dyeing commercially spun yarns but wasn't entirely happy with the fibers or the spinning. I wanted to make the yarn I'd been dreaming of. Since I had a background in production & textiles, I knew how to talk about the yarn & wanted in technical terms blends so I started approaching mills to custom spin for me with wool I had sourced directly from the people who raised it.

What keeps you on this path?

Getting to see finished projects people made & hearing that they are as happy with the yarn as I am is really satisfying. Working with local farms & mills has allowed me to meet so many people that are passionate about what they are doing & proud of their products and that too makes me know I've made the right choice.

I feel so lucky to be doing what I do. Being able to make a product that isn't quite "finished" until someone else adds their love & creativity to it is the most amazing job in the world. Getting notes from my customers or seeing the projects at fiber fests gets me through the hard days—and running a small business there are definitely hard days—but their smiling faces bring me back to why I do this.

Project #19

RONDOUT

Ladies Cardigan

DETAILS

YARN

Jill Draper Makes Stuff Windham
(100% merino wool, 113g, 220 yds/201m)
Color Vintage Denim, 4 (5, 5, 6, 6, 6, 7, 7, 8) skeins

FINISHED MEASUREMENTS

XS (S, M, L, XL, 2X, 3X, 4X, 5X)
Bust circumference: 34 (38, 42, 46, 50, 54, 58, 62, 66) inches
To fit bust: 30 (34, 38, 42, 46, 49, 54, 58, 62) inches, with 4 inches of
positive ease
Sample shown in S

RECOMMENDED NEEDLES

US size 7 (4.5 mm) needles, 32-inch circular and DPNs, or long circular
needles for magic loop

NOTIONS

Tapestry needle, stitch marker, stitch holder

GAUGE

18 stitches and 28 rows = 4 inches x 4 inches in (k1, p1) ribbing
28 rows/rounds = 4 inches x 4 inches in Mistake Rib Stitch Pattern

Introduction

*The variety of blues in this yarn remind me of changes the sky goes
through as afternoon slips into evening. This cozy open-front cardigan
is perfect to slip on for a twilight stroll.*

PATTERN

Mistake Rib Stitch Pattern (worked flat)

Row 1 (RS): k all sts

Row 2 (WS): (k1, p1) to end

Rows 3-8: Repeat Rows 1-2

Row 9: k all sts

Row 10: (p1, k1) to end

Rows 11-16: Repeat Rows 9-10

Mistake Rib Stitch Pattern (worked in the round)

Round 1: k all sts

Round 2: (p1, k1) to end

Rounds 3-8: Repeat Rounds 1-2

Round 9: k all sts

Round 10: (k1, p1) to end

Rounds 11-16: Repeat Rounds 9-10

Short rows worked within (k1, p1) ribbing are used to shape the yoke of the sweater. On the rows following a short row, when you come to a wrapped stitch, lift wrap off of the next stitch, place it on the left needle, and knit or purl the stitch together with the stitch it wraps.

Yoke

Cast on 33 (33, 35, 39, 39, 43, 43, 49, 49) sts.

Row 1 (RS): (k1, p1) to last st, k1.

Row 2 (WS): (p1, k1) to last st, p1.

Left Front V-Neck Short Rows

Row 3: Work 5 (5, 7, 11, 11, 5, 5, 11, 11) sts in pattern, pm, W&T.

Row 4: sm, work in pattern to end.

Row 5: Work in pattern to marker, rm, work wrapped st, work 2 (2, 2, 2, 2, 3, 3, 3, 3) more sts in pattern, pm, W&T.

Row 6: sm, work in pattern to end.

Rows 7-22: Repeat rows 5 and 6 eight more times.

Work 2 (2, 4, 2, 2, 2, 2, 2, 4) rows in pattern, hiding wraps as you come to them.

Left Shoulder Short Row Shaping

Row 1: Work 10 (10, 12, 12, 12, 16, 16, 16, 16) sts in pattern, W&T.

Rows 2, 4, and 6: Work in pattern to end.

Row 3: Work 21 (21, 23, 25, 25, 29, 29, 32, 32) sts in pattern, W&T.

Row 5: Work 32 (32, 34, 38, 38, 42, 42, 49, 49) sts in pattern, W&T.

Rows 7-8: Work two rows in pattern, hiding wraps.

Repeat rows 1-8, 13 (15, 17, 19, 21, 24, 26, 29, 31) more times.

Work 0 (0, 4, 4, 12, 4, 12, 0, 4) rows in pattern.

Right Shoulder Short Row Shaping

Rows 1 and 2: Work two rows in pattern.
Row 3: Work 32 (32, 34, 38, 38, 42, 42, 49, 49) sts in pattern, W&T.
Rows 4, 6, and 8: Work in pattern to end.
Row 3: Work 21 (21, 23, 25, 25, 29, 29, 32, 32) sts in pattern, W&T.
Row 7: Work 10 (10, 12, 12, 12, 16, 16, 16, 16) sts in pattern, W&T.

Work rows 1-8, 13 (15, 17, 19, 21, 24, 26, 29, 31) more times.

Work 2 (2, 4, 2, 2, 2, 2, 2, 4) rows in pattern, hiding wraps as you come to them.

Right front V-Neck Short Rows

Row 1: Work 32 (32, 34, 38, 38, 42, 42, 48, 48) sts in pattern, W&T.
Row 2: Work 3 (3, 3, 3, 3, 4, 4, 4, 4) sts in pattern, pm, work in pattern to end.
Row 3: Work in pattern to marker, rm, W&T
Row 4: Work 3 (3, 3, 3, 3, 4, 4, 4, 4) sts in pattern, pm, work in pattern to end.
Rows 5-20: Repeat rows 3 and 4 eight more times.

Work 2 rows in pattern, hiding wraps as you come to them.

Bind off all sts.

Body

With RS facing, starting at the bottom left of the yoke, pick up and knit 174 (196, 214, 240, 258, 292, 318, 340, 358) sts along the bottom edge of the yoke.

Set-up Row (WS): (k1, p1) to end.

Sleeve Separation Row (RS): k22 (27, 30, 34, 37, 42, 45, 48, 52), place next 36 (38, 40, 44, 48, 56, 62, 66, 68) sts onto a stitch holder, cast on 12 (12, 14, 14, 18, 18, 20, 22, 24) sts, k58 (66, 74, 84, 88, 96, 104, 112, 118), place next 36 (38, 40, 44, 48, 56, 62, 66, 68) sts onto a stitch holder, cast on 12 (12, 14, 14, 18, 18, 20, 22, 24) sts, k to end. 126 (144, 162, 180, 198, 216, 234, 252, 270) sts

Work rows 4-16 of Mistake Rib Stitch Pattern, then work rows 1-16 of Mistake Rib Stitch Pattern 5 (5, 6, 6, 6, 6, 6, 6, 6) times.

Sizes XS (S, -, -, -, 2X, 3X, 4X, 5X) only

Work rows 1-8 of Mistake Rib Stitch Pattern once more.

Hem Ribbing
Sizes XS (S, -, -, -, 2X, 3X, 4X, 5X)
Next Row: (p1, k1) to end.

Repeat last row seven more times.

Bind off all sts in pattern.

Sizes (-, M, L, XL, -, -, -, -)
Next Row: (k1, p1) to end.

Repeat last row seven more times.

Bind off all sts in pattern.

Sleeves

Left sleeve
Pick up and knit 12 (12, 14, 14, 18, 18, 20, 22, 24) sts from the underarm cast on edge, place the 36 (38, 40, 44, 48, 56, 62, 66, 68) sts from the stitch holder on to a needle and knit all sts from the needle, pm, and join in the round.
48 (50, 54, 58, 66, 74, 82, 88, 92) sts

Starting with round 4 (12, 4, 4, 12, 4, 12, 4, 4), work in Mistake Rib Stitch Pattern for 41 (33, 27, 31, 33, 35, 57, 47, 39) rounds.

Decreases
Decrease Round: k2tog, work in pattern to last 2 sts, ssk. 2 sts decreased

Continuing in pattern, repeat Decrease Round every 12 (12, 10, 10, 8, 6, 4, 4, 4) rounds, 5 (6, 8, 8, 10, 14, 16, 19, 21) more times. 36 (36, 36, 40, 44, 44, 48, 48, 48) sts.
Work 11 (11, 9, 9, 9, 5, 3, 3, 3) rounds in pattern.

Cuff Ribbing
Sizes XS (S, -, -, -, 2X, 3X, 4X, 5X)
Next Round: (p1, k1) to end.

Repeat last round seven more times.

Bind off all sts in pattern.

Sizes (-, M, L, XL, -, -, -, -)
Next Round: (k1, p1) to end.

Repeat last round seven more times.

Loosely bind off all sts in pattern.

Right Sleeve
Place the 36 (38, 40, 44, 48, 56, 62, 66, 68) sts from the stitch holder on to a needle and knit all sts from the needle, pick up and knit 12 (12, 14, 14, 18, 18, 20, 22, 24) sts from the underarm cast on edge, pm and join in the round. 48 (50, 54, 58, 66, 74, 82, 88, 92) sts

Work the remainder of the sleeve same as left sleeve.

Pockets

Left Pocket
Cast on 32 (32, 32, 34, 34, 34, 36, 36, 36) sts.
Starting with row 1, work 16 rows of Mistake Rib Stitch Pattern.

Pocket Slant
Row 1 (RS): sl 1, p1, k1, p1, ssk, work in pattern to end. 1 st decreased
Row 2: Work in pattern to last 5 sts, p1, (k1, p1) twice.

Repeat Rows 1 and 2 thirty more times.
Bind off all sts in pattern.

Right Pocket

Cast on 32 (32, 32, 34, 34, 34, 36, 36, 36) sts.

Starting with row 9, work 16 rows of Mistake Rib Stitch Pattern.

Pocket Slant

Row 1 (RS): Work in pattern to last 6 sts remain, k2tog, (p1, k1) twice. 1 st decreased
Row 2: l 1, (k1, p1) twice, work in pattern to end.
Repeat Rows 1 and 2 thirty more times.
Bind off all sts in pattern.

Line pockets up so that the bottom edge of the pocket meets the ribbing. Sew pockets onto sweater body using the mattress stitch.

Front Band

Cast on 15 sts.
Row 1 (RS): Sl1, (p1, k1) to end.
Row 2 (WS): (p1, k1) to last st, p1.

Work in pattern as established for 106 (106, 114, 114, 114, 122, 122, 122, 122) more rows.

Row 3: Work in pattern to last 3 sts, pm, k1, p1, k1.
Rows 4: Work in pattern to end.
Row 5: sl1, (p1, k1) to 1 st before marker, p1, M1, sm, k1, p1, k1. 1 st increased

Rows 6: p1, k1, p1, sm, p1, (k1, p1) to end.
Row 7: sl1, (p1, k1) to marker, M1, sm, k1, p1, k1. 1 st increased
Rows 8: p1, k1, p1, sm, (k1, p1) to end.
Work rows 5-8 five more times. 27 sts

Work in pattern for 114 (122, 144, 164, 180, 196, 204, 220, 232) rows.

Row 9: sl1, (p1, k1) to 2 sts before marker, ssk, sm, work in pattern to end. 1 st decreased
Row 10: Work in pattern to end .
Row 11: sl1, (p1, k1) to 2 sts before marker, ssp, sm, work in pattern to end. 1 st decreased
Row 12: Work in pattern to end.
Work rows 9-12 five more times. 15 sts

Work in pattern as established for 110 (110, 118, 118, 118, 126, 126, 126, 126) rows.
Bind off all sts in pattern.

Seaming

Pin the front band to the body of the sweater, taking care to align the beginning of the increase and decrease sections of the band with the point where the yoke ends and the body starts. Using the mattress stitch, sew front band onto sweater body.

Finishing

Weave in all ends and block according to the schematic.

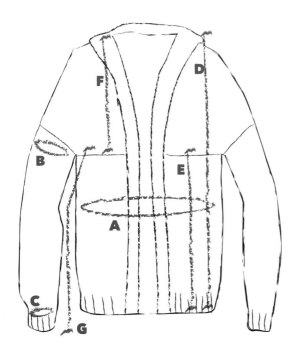

A: 34 (38, 42, 46, 50, 54, 58, 62, 66) inches

B: 10.75 (11.25, 12, 13, 14.5, 16.5, 18, 19.5, 20.5) inches

C: 8 (8, 8, 8.75, 9.75, 9.75, 10.5, 10.5, 10.5) inches

D: 22.75 (22.75, 24.25, 25.25, 25.25, 27.5, 27.5, 28.5, 28.5) inches

E: 15.75 (15.75, 16.75, 16.75, 16.75, 18, 18, 18, 18) inches

F: 7 (7, 7.5, 8.5, 8.5, 9.5, 9.5, 10.5, 10.5) inches

G: 17.5 (18, 18, 18.5, 18.5, 19, 19, 19.5, 19.5) inches

American Yarn File #15

DONE ROVING YARNS

Charlotte, Maine

Paula Farrar

What led you to your current path?

25 years ago I bought my first bred ewe. I brought her home in the cab of my husband's pickup. Of course, you know what a nervous ewe will do and of course you know who happily did that cleaning job. I bought two more bred ewes to start my flock. I was so happy when they all birthed out twin ewe lambs. That was my sign that I had missed my calling as a shepherdess. Our small flock grew into 75 breeding ewes and a full working fiber processing mill. I absolutely loved my new job of working with fiber from all types of farmers all over the U. S. and Canada as well as my own. Most years we were processing 2-3 tons of fiber. We marketed our own mill-spun yarns as well as uniquely dyed roving and needlefelting kits.

In 2008, our farm life changed immensely with a dog attack that ruined our breeding stock and a major health event that made it impossible for my husband to continue with our farming operation. So, our current path to Done Roving Yarns was born of the necessity to change. We redesigned and developed our yarn sales piece of our business plan to create our current hand-dyed yarn manufacturing operation.

What keeps you on this path?

We are proud of the company we have built based on our philosophy of maintaining an extremely high domestic product line. When we were researching for our niche, we discovered few companies offering domestic lines unless they were farm-based and shared a similarity to our background. This began our process of focusing on a domestic line in a manufacturing setting—which did not exist elsewhere at that time. Furthermore, we are proud of our extremely quick turnaround while keeping quality in the forefront. Along with our top-notch customer service we have a job to go to daily that we are not only proud of, but enjoy the atmosphere we have created.

What would you like people to know about you?

We do not use any harsh chemicals.
We are family run in a small rural community.
The owners are always in.
We are hands on with all of our products.
We are always creating something new.
We follow a lean manufacturing model that eliminates the waste of time, resources and dollars.

Project #20
SEBAGO

Infinity Cowl

DETAILS

YARN
Done Roving Yarns Frolicking Feet
(100% superwash merino wool, 480 yds / 438 m per 113g)
Color Blue Jeans, 2 skeins

FINISHED MEASUREMENTS
58 inches circumference x 11 inches wide

RECOMMENDED NEEDLES
US size 4 (3.5 mm) needles
Second needle US size 4 (3.5 mm) or smaller, for grafting

NOTIONS
Crochet hook, waste yarn, tapestry needle, 2 stitch markers

GAUGE
27 stitches and 48 rows = 4 inches x 4 inches in garter stitch
(Gauge is not critical for this project but will affect yardage)

Introduction

Blues and greens are my favorite colors, and they are artfully blended in this yarn. I wanted to make a simple design that would show off the way the colors play against one another over the length of the garment. The open mesh creates a draping fabric and gives the final cowl an elegant impression.

PATTERN

Cast on

With the waste yarn and crochet hook, chain 66 sts. Using the working needle and main yarn, pick up and knit 1 st in each bump on the crochet chain. 66 sts

Body

Row 1 (RS): (sl1 wyib) 3 times, k9, pm, k to last 12 sts, pm, k to end.

Row 2 (WS): (sl1 wyif) 3 times, k to last 3 sts slipping markers as you come to them, p3.

Rows 3-8: Repeat Rows 1 and 2 three times.

Row 9: (sl1 wyib) 3 times, k9, sm, *k2tog, yo, repeat from * to marker, sm, k to end.

Row 10: (sl1 wyif) 3 times, k9, sm, *k2tog, yo, repeat from * to marker, sm, k9, p3.

Rows 11-128: Repeat rows 9 and 10 fifty-nine times, or until you have a total of 60 garter ridges.

Row 129: (sl1 wyib) 3 times, k to end, slipping markers as you come to them.

Row 130: (sl1 wyif) 3 times, k to last 3 sts slipping markers as you come to them, p3.

Rows 131-136: Repeat rows 129 and 130 three times

Work rows 1-136 three more times (for a total of 4 lace sections).

Work rows 1-134 once more.

Grafting

Undo the crochet chain and place the 66 provisionally cast on sts onto another needle. Make sure not to twist the work.

Using the Kitchener grafting technique, graft the first three sts on both needles using the stockinette graft, work the next 60 sts on both needles using the garter stitch graft, work the remaining 3 sts on both needles using the stockinette graft.

Techniques and References

Grafting

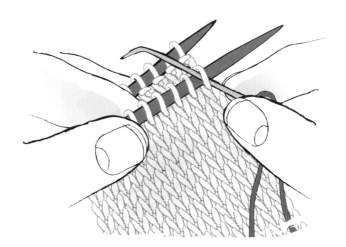

Grafting is magical. It allows knitters to create pieces that seemingly have no beginning and no end. Anything can be grafted. Some things are more tricky than others, but I hope to take a lot of the guess work out of it for you with this tutorial.

To begin for all types of grafting, undo the crochet cast on and place the provisional cast on sts onto another needle. Position the needles so that the needle with the cast on sts is held at the back and the needle with the sts just worked is held at the front (This method is a bit different, since other sources have the cast on sts held in the front, and the sts just worked held at the back).

Stockinette Grafting

Start by inserting the tapestry needle from the front to the back of the first st on the back needle.

Next insert the tapestry needle from the back to the front on the first st on the front needle.

*Insert the tapestry needle back to front on the first st of the back needle and slip it off of the needle.

Insert the tapestry needle front to back in the next st on the back needle.

On the front needle, insert the tapestry needle front to back in the first st and then slip the st off of the needle.

Insert the tapestry needle back to front in the next st on front needle.

Repeat from asterisk until all sts have been worked.

Reverse Stockinette Grafting

Start by inserting the tapestry needle from the back to the front of the first st on the back needle.

Next insert the tapestry needle from the front to the back on the first st on the front needle.

*Insert the tapestry needle front to back on the first st of the back needle and slip it off of the needle.

Insert the tapestry needle back to front in the next st on the back needle.

On the front needle, insert the tapestry needle back to front in the first st and then slip the st off of the needle.

Insert the tapestry needle front to back in the next st on front needle.

Repeat from asterisk until all sts have been worked.

Garter Stitch Grafting

Start by inserting the tapestry needle from the back to the front of the first st on the back needle.

Next insert the tapestry needle from the back to the front on the first st on the front needle.

*Insert the tapestry needle front to back on the first st of the back needle and slip it off of the needle.

Insert the tapestry needle back to front in the next st on the back needle.
On the front needle, insert the tapestry needle front to back in the first st and then slip the st off of the needle.

Insert the tapestry needle back to front in the next st on front needle.

Repeat from asterisk until all sts have been worked.

(k1, p1) Rib Grafting

Start by inserting the tapestry needle from the back to the front of the first st on the back needle.

Next insert the tapestry needle from the back to the front on the first st on the front needle.

*Insert the tapestry needle back to front on the first st of the back needle and slip it off of the needle.

Insert the tapestry needle front to back in the next st on the back needle.

On the front needle, insert the tapestry needle front to back in the first st and then slip the st off of the needle.

Insert the tapestry needle front to back in the next st on front needle.

Insert the tapestry needle front to back in the first st of the back needle and then slip the st off.
Insert the tapestry needle back to front in the next st on the back needle.

On the front needle, insert the tapestry needle back to front in the first st and then slip the st off of the needle.

Insert the tapestry needle back to front in the next st on front needle.

Repeat from asterisk until all sts have been worked.

Switching Stitch Patterns While Grafting

Two of the patterns in this book call for using more than one stitch pattern while grafting to finish a piece. The instructions given for grafting have been written in a way that makes this possible.

The patterns say to graft X stitches in a stitch pattern, then graft Y stitches in a different stitch pattern, and finally graft X stitches in the beginning stitch pattern.

The way to accomplish this is to start at the beginning of the instructions for the first stitch pattern. Work the repeat of the stitch pattern (from the * to the point it says to repeat) until the required number of stitches have been dropped from the needle.

Begin working the next stitch pattern from the * and repeat from the * until the required number of stitches have been dropped from the needle.

Finally return to the beginning stitch pattern and work from the * until the required number of stitches have been dropped from the needle.

References

Steeking

There are various methods for creating a steek. Since they involve slicing up your hard work, the idea of making one can be very scary. This is why I wanted to provide you with a few different resources to be able to make an informed decision about which method is best for you. These are just a few options and you will be sure to find more online.

I learned the method I chose for my steek from watching Ragga Eiríksdóttir's Craftsy video. I chose it because I liked how she used a purl stitch to mark where she wanted to cut the steek.

Eunny Jang explains three different steeks in a tutorial from Knitting Daily TV. You can view the tutorial on YouTube.

Wendy D Johnson wrote a fantastic tutorial with pictures on how to use a sewing machine to create a steek for the online magazine Knitty.
http://knitty.com/ISSUEspring03/FEATsteeks.html

For general knitting information on knitting, here are a few resources that I have always found helpful.

Knitty.com

Knitty is a great resource for information on how to knit as well as a place to find new and interesting patterns, cool knitting gear, information on spinning yarn, and articles about knitting.

Purlbee.com

The Purl Bee features a variety of beautifully photographed knitting projects as well as other craft projects. The great thing about the knitting projects listed on their site is that they also have picture tutorials on how to complete the more difficult points of the projects.

Vogueknitting.com

This is the online extension of the magazine VOGUEknitting. On their website you can find information about the latest issue of the magazine as well as a list of online learning resources, knitting how-tos, events, and other resources.

Knittinghelp.com

If you are a beginner, this website provides a information on the basics that are essential to learning to knit. There are videos as well as picture tutorials.

Craftsy.com

Craftsy is a great resource for all things craft. They provide online learning for various knitting techniques with a variety of wonderful instructors.

Resources

Harrisville Designs
http://harrisville.com

Brooklyn Tweed
https://www.brooklyntweed.com

Manuosh
https://www.manuosh.com

Mountain Meadows Wool
http://www.mountainmeadowwool.com

Element Effects
https://www.fancytigercrafts.com

ElsaWool
http://www.wool-clothing.com

Spincycle Yarns
http://spincycleyarns.com

Rock Garden Alpacas
http://rockgardenalpacas.blogspot.com

Sheeps and Peeps Farm
http://sheepsandpeepsfarm.blogspot.com

A Wing and A Prayer Farm
http://www.woolfulmercantile.com

Jill Draper
http://www.jilldraper.com

Lakes Yarn & Fiber
http://www.lakesyarn.com

Pigeonroof Studios
http://www.pigeonroofstudios.com

Frabjous Fibers
http://frabjousfibers.com

Done Roving Yarns
http://www.doneroving.com

Additional Materials

Knitpicks.com has a great variety of knitting tools and notions. For the projects in this book I used a set of KnitPicks Options Interchangeable Circular Knitting Needles for which also I purchased the Jumbo Interchangeable Birchwood needle tips that I used to knit the super bulky yarn projects. On this site you can also find the Fiber Trends Slipper Bottoms.

Acknowledgements

Firstly, I want to thank all of the yarn producers who so graciously agreed to be apart of this project. Your beautiful yarns are a constant inspiration.

Glenn, thank for guiding and supporting me, and giving me the opportunity to write.

Tsukuru, thank you for lending your excellent eye for design and turning this project into a beautiful book.

Chaitanya, you have been indispensable. I really appreciate all the time and effort you put into this project.

Emma, your fleet fingers were a blessing to me. Thank you for lending your hands.

And thanks to Soshi, Mom, and Susi for supporting me through the process.

ANNA SUDO

is a graduate of the Kansas City Art Institute. After spending a decade in Japan, she returned to the Midwest and rediscovered American yarns. She found that showcasing the producers and quality of these yarns in her original designs was an intuitive way to reconnect with her own roots. She is currently based in Kansas City, MO.